Plough Quarterly

BREAKING GROUND FOR A RENEWED WORLD

Summer 2016, Number 9

Artists: Salvador Dalí, Wassily Kandinsky, Juan Rizi, Marianne Stokes, Francisco de Zurbarán, Kim Dong-sung, Christian Schussele

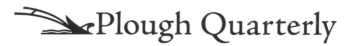

Plough Quarterly

BREAKING GROUND FOR A RENEWED WORLD

www.plough.com

Plough Quarterly features original stories, ideas, and culture to inspire everyday faith and action. Starting from the conviction that the teachings and example of Jesus can transform and renew our world, we aim to apply them to all aspects of life, seeking common ground with all people of goodwill regardless of creed. The goal of *Plough Quarterly* is to build a living network of readers, contributors, and practitioners so that, in the words of Hebrews, we may "spur one another on toward love and good deeds."

This magazine is published by Plough, the publishing house of the Bruderhof, an international movement of Christian communities whose members are called to follow Jesus together in the spirit of the Sermon on the Mount and of the first church in Jerusalem, sharing all talents, income, and possessions (Acts 2 and 4). Bruderhof communities, which include both families and single people from a wide range of backgrounds, are located in the United States, England, Germany, Australia, and Paraguay. Visitors are welcome at any time. To learn more about the Bruderhof's faith, history, and daily life, or to find a community near you to arrange a visit, see *www.bruderhof.com*.

Plough Quarterly includes contributions that we believe are worthy of our readers' consideration, whether or not we fully agree with them. Views expressed by contributors are their own and do not necessarily reflect the editorial position of Plough or of the Bruderhof communities.

Editors: Peter Mommsen, Sam Hine, Maureen Swinger. Art director: Emily Alexander. Online editor: Erna Albertz. Contributing editors: Sung Hoon Park, Charles E. Moore, Christopher Zimmerman, Chungyon Won. Founding Editor: Eberhard Arnold (1883–1935).

Plough Quarterly No. 9: All Things in Common?
Published by Plough Publishing House, ISBN 978-0-87486-785-5
Copyright © 2016 by Plough Publishing House. All rights reserved.

Scripture quotations (unless otherwise noted) are from the New Revised Standard Version Bible, copyright © 1989 the Division of Christian Education of the National Council of the Churches of Christ in the United States of America. Used by permission. All rights reserved.

Front cover: photograph by Clare Stober. Inside front cover: Painting by Salvador Dalí (1904–89) / National Gallery of Art, Washington DC, USA / Bridgeman Images / © Salvador Dalí, Gala-Salvador Dalí Foundation/Artists Rights Society (ARS), New York.

Editorial Office
PO Box 398
Walden, NY 12586
T: 845.572.3455
info@plough.com

Subscriber Services
PO Box 345
Congers, NY 10920-0345
T: 800.521.8011
subscriptions@plough.com

United Kingdom
Brightling Road
Robertsbridge
TN32 5DR
T: +44(0)1580.883.344

Australia
4188 Gwydir Highway
Elsmore, NSW
2360 Australia
T: +61(0)2.6723.2213

Plough Quarterly (ISSN 2372-2584) is published quarterly by Plough Publishing House, PO Box 398, Walden, NY 12586.
Individual subscription $32 per year in the United States; Canada add $8, other countries add $16.
Periodicals postage paid at Walden, NY 12586 and at additional mailing offices.
POSTMASTER: Send address changes to *Plough Quarterly*, PO Box 345, Congers, NY 10920-0345.

All Things in Common?

Dear Reader,

"From each according to his ability, to each according to his need." Since the collapse of Soviet-style communism, it's been easy to dismiss this motto, made famous by Karl Marx in 1875, as a stale relic of failed socialism. Yet in 2016, in an astounding twist, the once-toxic term *socialism* is being rehabilitated by mainstream politicians in Europe and the United States. According to polls, a majority of American millennials say they prefer socialism to free-market capitalism.

How deep this current runs is open to question. True socialism is a demanding, even ascetic, creed, while today's version is often long on vague empathy and short on self-sacrifice. Still, the widespread hunger for a world where people live in solidarity, sharing their resources and lives in dedication to the common good, should give Christians pause. After all, this was our idea first.

Immediately after Pentecost, the Book of Acts tells us, the first church in Jerusalem celebrated its newfound unity in the Holy Spirit by . . . abolishing private property. "Now the whole group of those who believed were of one heart and soul, and no one claimed private ownership of any possessions, but everything they owned was held in common . . . and it was distributed to each as any had need" (Acts 4:32–35). Even if historical criticism is right to view this account as idealized, the fact remains: for the apostolic community, a life of economic sharing was the first sign of the church. In this, Acts is simply echoing Jesus' Sermon on the Mount, Paul's appeals for *koinonia*, and before them, the Hebrew prophets' calls for repentance and the Torah's requirements for the Jubilee.

How faithfully has the church lived out this biblical vision? Not very, it's tempting to reply. To that extent, G. K. Chesterton's remark holds true that "the Christian ideal has not been tried and found wanting. It has been found difficult; and left untried."

Yet that's not the whole story. Two millennia of back-to-the-gospel movements, from monastics to radical Reformers, testify to a vibrant communal tradition (page 42). Recently, this impulse has reemerged under labels such as "slow church," "new monasticism," or "missional church."

As a member of a community that has shared all things in common since 1920, I'm naturally enthusiastic about such stirrings. Still, great caution is in order. Stanley Hauerwas puts it well when he says, "Community is dangerous": dangerous whenever it is no longer a fellowship gathered around Jesus (page 32). For examples, we need look no farther than political communism and fascism. We who live in an isolated age that craves togetherness are hardly exempt from similar temptations, in religion as in politics.

That is why in this issue we draw on the wisdom of men and women whose lives in community are centered passionately on Christ. For them, as for the first church in Jerusalem, community is not a new law but rather the fruit of overflowing love between brothers and sisters gripped by the Holy Spirit. Then, as Eberhard Arnold writes (page 22), "our whole life in all its aspects becomes a symbol of the future of humankind in the coming kingdom of God." Isn't this the gospel's answer to our world's horrors and its yearnings?

Warm greetings,

Peter

Peter Mommsen

Editor

Lovis Corinth, *Woman Reading*, 1888

Image from WikiArt (public domain)

Bringing Home the War

On Michael Yandell's "Hope in the Void," Spring 2016: This very helpful article shows how simply calling our veterans heroes cuts short their experiences and keeps all of us from looking honestly at the impact of war. We absolve ourselves of our own responsibility for war by deeming all veterans heroes, which doesn't capture everything that happened during war. I appreciate Yandell's call for Americans to stop pretending that our lives are not interconnected with global violence. And I take to heart his appeal for us to be genuinely present with veterans. We aren't doing a service by "unhappening what has really happened." Instead, we must make space for people's pain and suffering, to allow them to find the path to healing, hope, and honesty.

Allison Lattin, Albany, NY

For us military wives taking care of our husbands, it is no cakewalk – in fact, it's like a war zone at times. Praying alone won't help – when the soldiers come home, you have to get professional help for the consequences of war. Yet how important it is to have a spouse that stays with you and understands what you are going through. *Juliana Benoit, Easley, SC*

My father felt war guilt from World War II; as a bomber pilot he knew that innocent people are sometimes casualties of bombs. He had to come to terms with all that war entails – learn to live with his demons, so to speak. How are military chaplains helping here? Too often, their training is not Bible-based but rather Zen-like and universalist in its approach to the person in need. Yes, their task is to listen. But isn't it also to give a witness to Jesus?

Cathy Madden, Dallas, TX

Views on Syria

On Navid Kermani's "Love in Syria: Learning from Jacques Mourad," Spring 2016: As we absorb the powerful message of this article, we dare not ignore ironies, inconsistencies, and errors in his account.

Kermani lumps the government's expulsion of Paolo Dall'Oglio together with acts of violence, even though the expulsion of such an outspoken supporter of insurrection was surely an act of mercy. He speaks not a word of criticism of the al-Qaeda-led insurgents who have constituted the heart of the violent opposition to the Syrian government. He ignores the fact that U.N. Secretary Kofi Annan nearly ended this terrible war in the spring of 2012, only to see his effort aborted by the Western demand that "Assad must go." And he speaks not a word of how ISIS has been empowered by the actions of the US-led coalition and Western media.

In short, Kermani rightfully denounces the cynicism of the West, but fails to plumb its depths. Remarkable, isn't it, how his prayers for the people of Syria and Iraq were being answered as he spoke by Russia's vigorous entry into the war in support of the Syrian government? *Berry Friesen, Lancaster, PA*

I admire the efforts being made by Father Jacques Mourad and others to promote and maintain Christian–Muslim relations. While I can understand Fr. Jacques's frustration when he says, "We have been abandoned by the Christian world – we mean nothing to them," I would like to assure him that many ordinary Christians are actively working to alleviate the plight of the suffering people in Syria and other affected Middle East countries. The Catholic charity with which I've worked as a volunteer for over twenty years has provided substantial aid and continues to assist in Syria, Lebanon, and Iraq. More importantly, at our midday Angelus prayer here in Sutton, we pray daily for the suffering people of the Middle East, be they Christian or Muslim. In this way, we remain in solidarity with our suffering brothers and sisters.

Mervyn Maciel, Sutton, UK

The Face of the Poor

On Neil Shigley's "Invisible People," Spring 2016: It is in loving and gazing at the face of the poor and homeless that we will see Christ, who loved them till death. Fear causes us to avoid connecting with them, but love conquers fear; therefore, we should pray for the courage to love. *Luz Lopez-Dee, Vancouver, BC*

Strangers No More

On Sheera Hinkey's "Snapshots from Lesbos," Winter 2016: This January a family of five Kurdish Syrians was dropped off at our farm in British Columbia, where my family and I live in Christian community with five other families. We are committed to caring for the land and each other, and to showing hospitality to those in need, though this has tended to be people in our own neighborhood. When we saw the crisis and plight of those in Syria we knew we must respond. So this family, who were strangers to Canada and to us, joined our community. One obvious barrier was language, but we have been amazed how quickly one can communicate without language. There were

the challenges of helping them find language training, schools for the kids, health insurance, and transportation. But none of these small inconveniences can compare to the unbelievable blessing it has been to have them on the farm. They understand community – it is in their DNA – and they have enhanced our community. We are learning from them and their culture. They are strangers no more. They are family. *Craig Smith, Surrey, BC*

Teaching the Faith

We recently used *Plough's* Winter 2015 issue ("Childhood") at the annual faculty retreat day with our elementary school teachers. The articles "Discovering Reverence" by Johann Christoph Arnold and "What's the Point of a Christian Education?" by Christiaan Alting von Geusau sparked a wonderful conversation about our responsibilities as Christian teachers. Von Geusau's words about friendship, faithfulness, formation, and freedom prompted us to develop several new strategies to further develop these virtues among our students. Please know how valuable your magazine is for so many of us who are striving along with you to educate young people to be true disciples of Jesus and brothers and sisters to each other.

Br. Timothy Driscoll, Uniondale, NY

Thoughts on Ploughing

Plough Quarterly is the richest publication I get these days. "Love in Syria" and "Hope in the Void" were world-class: insightful, stunning, deeply spiritual, provocative. The entire magazine is beautifully conceived and professionally executed. *Philip Yancey, Evergreen, CO*

We welcome letters to the editor. Letters and web comments may be edited for length and clarity, and may be published in any medium. Letters should be sent with the writer's name and address to letters@plough.com.

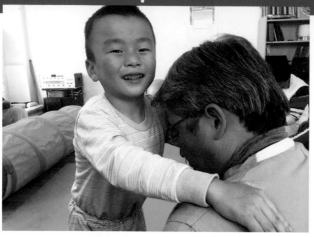

The Ignis Community in North Korea: Dr. Stephen Yoon helps children with cerebral palsy.

Serving Children in Pyongyang

Stephen Yoon, a doctor and chiropractor, spoke with *Plough* about his work caring for children with disabilities in North Korea. Dr. Yoon is a member of Ignis Community, one of the few openly Christian ministries operating in Pyongyang. An eight-member team in Pyongyang shares one vehicle and lives together in one house.

Working with other Ignis members, Dr. Yoon has spearheaded a program in Pyongyang to help children with cerebral palsy learn to walk. One of his wheelchair-bound patients dreamed of being able to walk to school with her friends. Dr. Yoon's treatment enabled her to do so and attracted government support for his work. The subsequent Pyongyang Spine Rehabilitation Center (PYSRC) is currently creating programs to train doctors who can then take what they have learned to other regions of North Korea. According to Dr. Yoon, prior to PYSRC there was virtually no treatment for cerebral palsy in the country.

In addition to caring for children with disabilities, Ignis Community also distributes food, medicine, and essentials such as footwear to rural areas of North Korea. "Despite the restrictions, we have been amazed by what we have been given freedom to do. And as long as we allow enough time to receive the proper permission, we have found that there is little we cannot do."

Poet in This Issue: Matthew Baker

See his poem "Rainfall" on page 31.

Sketch by Adam Wagner

A lifelong student of literature, philosophy, and languages, Rhode Island native Matthew J. Baker dropped out of high school and got a job working nights at a gas station so he would have more time to read. This he did for seven years, going on to become a distinguished Orthodox Christian theologian with degrees from St. Tikhon's Seminary, Holy Cross School of Theology, and Fordham University. Married and the father of six children, Baker was ordained to the priesthood of the Greek Orthodox Church in 2014. Only six weeks after being installed in his first parish, Holy Trinity Church of Norwich, Connecticut, he died in a snowstorm car accident on March 1, 2015. He was thirty-seven.

Homage Recognized

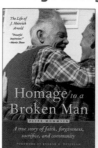

Homage to a Broken Man: The Life of J. Heinrich Arnold (Plough, 2015) won gold at the 2016 IPPY Awards, for best biography of the year from an independent publisher, and silver at the Independent Book Publishers Association's 2016 Benjamin Franklin Awards, for best religion book of the year. "A true story of faith, forgiveness, sacrifice, and community," *Homage to a Broken Man* is also a finalist for *Foreword Reviews'* Indiefab Award for best biography of the year. ⤳

Image courtesy of Katherine Baker. Photograph courtesy of Ignis Community

The God Who Heals

RICK WARREN

Pastor Warren, author of The Purpose Driven Life, *wrote this foreword to a new Plough book,* The God Who Heals: Words of Hope for a Time of Sickness, *by Johann Christoph Blumhardt and Christoph Friedrich Blumhardt.*

AT SOME POINT IN LIFE, every person will experience suffering, pain, and, eventually, death. It's inevitable. When it happens, how are we going to respond?

Many of us, even Christians, struggle with God's purpose when we are suddenly faced with a serious illness or terminal diagnosis. Our first response is to turn to God, asking him to spare us from the suffering. But what if his answer is not to heal us immediately but to perfect us through the suffering? Such a season can test our faith. But if we can surrender our will to his, through that pain God can deepen our faith, heal our soul, and restore our joy.

In their book, *The God Who Heals,* the Blumhardts remind us that physical healing is not God's greatest answer to prayer. True healing is trusting God even when we lack understanding. It's believing in the promises written in his Word, which renews our mind and lifts our spirit even as our body is failing. It's not giving in to our fears. It's about giving ourselves completely to Jesus. Whatever circumstance you are facing right now, this book of daily readings will help you focus on a closer relationship with Jesus, our one true spiritual healer.

When you go through deep valleys, God is there with you, walking alongside as you experience suffering. He knows it well. He's been there. He understands. As one who knows great pain, Jesus is our Great Comforter. In his First Letter to the Corinthians, the apostle Paul tells us that just as God comforts us in our troubles, so too we can comfort others. How will you respond to the pain in your life? Our faith tells us that Jesus is the source of victory even in the midst of suffering. That's because God doesn't waste a hurt. He can use that pain to direct us in the way he wants us to go, to reveal what's inside of us, to perfect us, and to make us more like himself. He is the Great Physician who specializes in bringing blessing out of pain.

Open up your life completely to him and get to know Jesus more intimately. Soak in these "words of hope for a time of sickness" by the Blumhardts and find healing strength for your soul. Hide God's word in your heart, surrender your will, and trust in God's promises. He will carry you through to eternity. You have his Word on it! ⤳

These sixty short daily reflections, each based on a verse from the Bible, will guide any believer facing serious sickness to a rock-solid trust in God. The Blumhardts, a father-son team of pastors renowned for their healing ministry, point us away from our troubles and toward a Savior who wants the best for each of us.

Plough, 2016, hardcover, 192 pages.

All Things in

Jerusalem, ca. AD 33: "They devoted themselves to the apostles'

And fear came upon every soul; and many wonders and signs were done through the apostles. And all who believed were together and had all things in common; and they sold their possessions and goods and distributed them to all, as any had need. And day by day, attending the temple together

Photograph by Clare Stober

Common.

teaching and fellowship, to the breaking of bread and the prayers.

and breaking bread in their homes, they partook of food with glad and generous hearts, praising God and having favor with all the people.

And the Lord added to their number day by day those who were being saved." Acts 2:42–47 (RSV)

Life Together

Beyond Sunday Religion and Social Activism

CHARLES E. MOORE

How would you go about destroying community, isolating people from one another and from a life shared with others? Over thirty years ago Howard Snyder asked this question and offered the following strategies: fragment family life, move people away from the neighborhoods where they grew up, set people farther apart by giving them bigger houses and yards, and separate the places people work from where they live.[1] In other words, "partition off people's lives into as many worlds as possible." To facilitate the process, get everyone his or her own car. Replace meaningful communication with television. And finally, cut down on family size and fill people's homes with things instead. The result? A post-familial, disconnected culture where self is king, relationships are thin, and individuals fend for themselves.

As a result, our culture – in the words of the writer Michael Frost – has become like an airport departure lounge, "full of people who don't belong where they currently find themselves and whose interactions with others are fleeting, perfunctory, and trivial."[2] Nobody belongs there, nobody is truly present, and nobody wants to be there. We're tourists who graze from one experience to another, nibbling here and sampling there, but with very little commitment to bind us to one another.

The disappearance of community has led to a plethora of human and social problems, which have been exposed and explored in countless books. But what can we do about it? Many social commentators have addressed the problem and continue to grapple with it. New structures of belonging have been proposed, many of which hold promise. But the real answer lies in the hands of God's people. We need more than new structures. We need a spirit-filled life that is capable of combatting the corrosive ideologies of our age. Only when the church lives out its original calling, as a contrast community and foretaste of God's coming reign, is there hope for the world. And there is hope. The Bible assures us that through faith in Jesus and by God's spirit a new kind of social existence is possible. Christ has defeated the principalities and powers that keep people apart. In him relationships can be healed and transformed. This is what being the church is all about.

Charles E. Moore is a member of the Bruderhof community and teaches at the Mount Academy in New York. He is the editor of a new Plough book, Called to Community: The Life Jesus Wants for His People, *from which the articles on pages 10–21 are taken.*

Committed followers of Christ from every corner of society and from all walks of life are responding to Christ's call to embody an integrated spirituality that encompasses the whole of life and is lived out with others. New intentional communities are emerging that bear witness to Christ's healing power. A radical renaissance is unfolding among disenchanted Christians who are no longer satisfied with either Sunday religion or social activism. Today's Christians want to be the church, to follow Christ together and demonstrate in their daily lives the radical, transforming love of God.

Of course, in a world in which family life is undermined and faithfulness and loyalty are old-fashioned concepts, living in community will not be easy. The broader culture rarely reinforces values such as fidelity, the common good, and social solidarity. It's everyone out for themselves. We're on our own, whether we like it or not. And yet for growing numbers of Christians this world, with its dominant ideology of expressive individualism, is not the final adjudicator of what is or is not possible, let alone desirable. The world Christ was born into was also splintered and confused; it was violent, factious, morally corrupt, spiritually bankrupt, full of tensions, and teeming with competing interests. Yet, into this world a brand new social order erupted. It caught everybody's attention, and eventually transformed the entire Roman pagan system.

It has been said that true community is all or nothing, and that communities which try to get there by degrees just get stuck. This may be true. And yet, much like a healthy marriage, it takes time and wisdom to build a community. It also takes very little to break and destroy a community. Perhaps this is one of the reasons why so few people dare to commit themselves to building a common life. As Henri Nouwen writes, fearful distance is awful, but fearful closeness, if not properly navigated, can turn into a nightmare.[3]

Thomas Merton once noted that living alone does not necessarily isolate people, and that

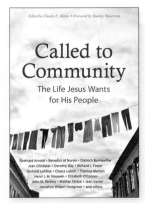

Called to Community
The Life Jesus Wants for His People
softcover, 381 pages
Plough, 2016

Spark group discussion with fifty-two readings on living in intentional Christian community.

Increasingly, today's Christians want to be the church – to follow Christ together in daily life.

Of course, such a life together with others isn't easy. The selections in this volume are written by people who have discovered in the nitty-gritty of daily life what it takes to establish, nurture, and sustain a Christian community over the long haul.

Contributors include Eberhard Arnold, Benedict of Nursia, Dietrich Bonhoeffer, Joan Chittister, Dorothy Day, David Janzen, Chiara Lubich, Thomas Merton, Henri J. M. Nouwen, John M. Perkins, Mother Teresa, Jean Vanier, and Jonathan Wilson-Hartgrove.

merely living together does not necessarily bring us into communion with one another.[4] So what is the key to communing with one another? Community as Christ intended it demands, if nothing else, a commitment to care for one another – to be our brother's and sister's keeper. Without simple deeds of love, community is not possible.

Dr. Paul Brand, who devoted himself to eliminating leprosy, was once working alone in an attic when he came across some boxes of skeletons that had been dug up from a monastery. He remembered a lecture he heard given by anthropologist Margaret Mead, who spent much of her life researching prehistoric peoples. She asked her audience, "What is the earliest sign of civilization? A clay pot? Iron? Tools? Agriculture?" No, she claimed, it was a healed leg bone. Brand recalls:

> She explained that such healings were never found in the remains of competitive, savage societies. There, clues of violence abounded: temples pierced by arrows, skulls crushed by clubs. But the healed femur showed that someone must have cared for the injured person – hunted on his behalf, brought him food, and served him at personal sacrifice. Savage societies could not afford such pity. I found similar evidence of healing in the bones from the churchyard. I later learned

that an order of monks had worked among the victims: their concern came to light five hundred years later in the thin lines of healing where infected bone had cracked apart or eroded and then grown back together.[5]

Community is all about helping each other – caring enough to invest oneself in the "thin lines of healing." There is no other way to have community. The apostle Paul wrote, "The only thing that counts is faith expressing itself through love" (Gal. 5:6). Words and ideas, forms and structures, can take us only so far. In the end, it's a matter of whether we will lay down our lives for one another. For Christ's followers, this is not just a matter of obedience but the distinguishing mark of our witness. Jesus says, "A new command I give you: Love one another. As I have loved you, so you must love one another. By this everyone will know that you are my disciples, if you love one another" (John 13:34–35). ✒

It's a matter of whether we will lay down our lives for one another.

1. Howard A. Snyder, *Liberating the Church: The Ecology of Church and Kingdom* (Downers Grove, IL: InterVarsity Press, 1983), 113–114.

2. Michael Frost, *Incarnate: The Body of Christ in an Age of Disengagement* (Downers Grove, IL: IVP Books, 2014), 16.

3. Henri J. M. Nouwen, *Lifesigns: Intimacy, Fecundity, and Ecstasy in Christian Perspective* (New York: Doubleday, 2013), 19.

4. Thomas Merton, *New Seeds of Contemplation* (New York: New Directions Books, 1972), 55.

5. Paul Brand and Philip Yancey, *Fearfully and Wonderfully Made* (Grand Rapids, MI: Zondervan, 1980), 68.

Solidarity

CHRISTOPH FRIEDRICH BLUMHARDT

For those who keep their eyes on God's kingdom, it is not only in the future – it is already coming into being in the present. And it is present, for this faith is today shaping a community of men and women, a society in which people strengthen each other toward this goal. Without such a society, how is faith possible? The kingdom of God must be foreshadowed in a human society. The apostle Paul calls this society the body of Christ, of which Christ is the head (1 Cor. 12:12–27). Peter calls it a building, where each stone fits the next so that the building becomes complete (1 Pet. 2:4–12). Jesus calls it his little flock, where all love one another, where each answers for the others and all answer for the one. As such, we are fighters for the future, through whom the earth must become bright. In this way God's kingdom comes into the present, just as it shall be in the future.

In order to form such a society in Christ there must be people who are resolute and free from anxiety. Right from the beginning, when the apostles began to preach, Christians sought this freedom from worry. But do not misunderstand this. You can't just say to your neighbor, "Don't worry!" When a person lives utterly alone and nobody is concerned about him, when other people kick him around or want nothing to do with him, when a person is excluded from everything that lends dignity to life, when there is nothing for him to do but earn his bread with much worry, toil, and burden, then it is a sin to say to him, "Don't worry!". . .

At present the whole world, including the wealthiest of nations, lies deep in worries and cares. But within the society and organism that proceeds from Christ, worries can and should cease. There we should care for one another. When the apostle Paul says, "Do not worry," he takes it for granted that these are people who are united by a bond of solidarity so that no one says anymore, "This is mine," but all say, "Our solidarity, our bond, must take away our worries. All that we share together must help each one of us and so rid us of anxiety." In this

> **Within a society that proceeds from Christ, worries can and should cease.**

Christoph Friedrich Blumhardt (1842–1919) was a German pastor and religious socialist.

way the kingdom of heaven comes. First it comes in a small flock free from anxiety. Thus Jesus teaches: "I tell you, do not worry about your life, what you will eat or drink; or about your body, what you will wear. . . . But seek first God's kingdom and his righteousness, and all these things will be given to you as well" (Matt. 6:25–34).

From the beginning, ever since Christ was born, people have sought such a society, a fellowship of the kingdom, free from cares and worries. There is an enormous strength when people stand together, when they unite in a communal way. The idea of private property falls away, and they are so bound together in the Spirit that each one says, "What I have belongs to the others, and if I should ever be in need, they will help me" (2 Cor. 8:13–15). This firm and absolute solidarity in a shared life where each is responsible for the other is the kind of life in which you can indeed say, "Do not worry!"

Time and again, people have attempted to live together in this way. Yet it has never come fully into being. And this is the reason why Christianity has become so weak.

For this reason I do not think much of "spiritual communities." They do not last. People are friends for a while, but it eventually ends. Anything that is going to last must have a much deeper foundation than some kind of spiritual experience. Unless we have community in the

Unless we have community in material things, we will never have it in spiritual matters.

flesh, in things material, we will never have it in spiritual matters (1 John 3:16–18). We are not mere spirits. We are human beings of flesh and blood. Every day we need to eat. We need clothing for every season. We must share our tools; we must work together; we must work communally and not each for himself. Otherwise we can never become one in the love of Christ, can never become the flock, the community of Jesus that stands up in the world and says, "Now things must become quite different. Now the individual must stop living for himself. Now a society of brothers and sisters must arise."

This is the way Jesus calls us to set aside our worries. Yet we Christians somehow expect people to have faith in the most impossible of situations, in conditions where they nearly perish in need and misery, where they exist in wretched hovels, hardly knowing how to keep the wolf from the door. And we come along and call out to them, "Simply believe!" To shout into this kind of distress, "Believe! Then everything will be added unto you – heaven awaits you!" is a demand that simply cannot be carried out (James 2:14–18). No, the kingdom of God must not be only a kingdom of the future. In Christ's church community we should strive to become united, and begin to become free in such a way that, at least in the circles where we love one another, cares cease. ⤙

Photograph by Kasia Lauwerijssen-Weglicka

Possessions

C.S. LEWIS

Of all the things that can come between people and poison life in community, possessiveness is perhaps the most common. In C. S. Lewis's The Screwtape Letters, *Screwtape, a senior demon, advises his inexperienced nephew, Wormwood, on how best to corrupt a human.*

My dear Wormwood,
. . . The sense of ownership in general is always to be encouraged. The humans are always putting up claims to ownership which sound equally funny in heaven and in hell, and we must keep them doing so. Much of the modern resistance to chastity comes from people's belief that they "own" their bodies – those vast and perilous estates, pulsating with the energy that made the worlds, in which they find themselves without their consent and from which they are ejected at the pleasure of Another! It is as if a royal child whom his father has placed, for love's sake, in titular command of some great province, under the real rule of wise counselors, should come to fancy he really owns the cities, the forests, and the corn, in the same way as he owns the bricks on the nursery floor.

We produce this sense of ownership not only by pride but by confusion. We teach them not to notice the different senses of the possessive pronoun – the finely graded differences that run from "my boots" through "my dog," "my servant," "my wife," "my father," "my master," and "my country," to "my God." They can be taught to reduce all these senses to that of "my boots," the "my" of ownership.

Even in the nursery a child can be taught to mean by "my teddy bear," not the old imagined recipient of affections to whom it stands in a special relation (for that is what the Enemy will teach them to mean if we are not careful), but "the bear I can pull to pieces if I like." And at the other end of the scale, we have taught people to say "my God" in a sense not really very different from "my boots," meaning "the God on whom I have a claim for my distinguished services and whom I exploit from the pulpit – the God I have done a corner in."

And all the time the joke is that the word "mine" in its fully possessive sense cannot be uttered by a human being about anything. In the long run either Our Father [the devil] or the Enemy will say "mine" of each thing that exists, and especially of each man. They will find out in the end, never fear, to whom their time, their souls, and their bodies really belong – certainly not to *them,* whatever happens. At present the Enemy says "mine" of everything on the pedantic, legalistic ground that he made it. Our Father hopes in the end to say "mine" of all things on the more realistic and dynamic ground of conquest.

Your affectionate uncle,
Screwtape

C. S. Lewis (1898–1963) was a British novelist and Christian apologist.

Deeds

JEAN VANIER

One of the signs that a community is alive can be found in material things. Cleanliness, furnishings, the way flowers are arranged and meals prepared, are among the things which reflect the quality of people's hearts. Some people may find material chores irksome; they would prefer to use their time to talk and be with others. They haven't yet realized that the thousand and one small things that have to be done each day, the cycle of dirtying and cleaning, were given by God to enable us to communicate through matter. Cooking and washing floors can become a way of showing our love for others. If we see the humblest task in this light, everything can become communion and so celebration – because it is celebration to be able to give.

It is important, too, to recognize the humble and material gifts that others bring and to thank them for them. Recognition of the gifts of others is essential in community. All it takes is a smile and two small words – "Thank you."

> When we put love into what we do, it becomes beautiful.

When we put love into what we do, it becomes beautiful, and so do the results. There is a lack of love in a dirty or untidy community. But the greatest beauty is in simplicity and lack of affectation, where everything is oriented toward a meeting of people among themselves and with God. The way we look after the house and garden shows whether we feel really at home, relaxed, and peaceful. The house is the nest; it is like an extension of the body. Sometimes we tend to forget the role of the environment in liberation and inner growth.

Our lives in L'Arche are disarmingly simple. We often say that half the day is taken up with dirtying things and the other half with cleaning up! That is not entirely true because we also have work, celebrations, meals, and prayer. But that does say something about the littleness and ordinariness of our lives.

Jean Vanier, born in 1928, is a French spiritual writer and the founder of the L'Arche community.

Photograph from clairlythgoe.co.uk.com

Differences

HENRI J. M. NOUWEN

Photograph by Devany Vickery-Davidson

When we give up our desires to be outstanding or different, when we let go of our need to have our own special niches in life, when our main concern is to be the same and to live out this sameness in solidarity, we are then able to see each other's unique gifts. Gathered together in common vulnerability, we discover how much we have to give each other. The Christian community is the opposite of a highly uniform group of people whose behavior has been toned down to a common denominator and whose originality has been dulled. On the contrary, the Christian community, gathered in common discipleship, is the place where individual gifts can be called forth and put into service for all. It belongs to the essence of this new togetherness that our unique talents are no longer objects of competition but elements of community, no longer qualities that divide but gifts that unite.

When we have discovered that our sense of self does not depend on our differences and that our self-esteem is based on a love much deeper than the praise that can be acquired by unusual performances, we can see our unique talents as gifts for others. Then, too, we will notice that the sharing of our gifts does not diminish our own value as persons but enhances it. In community, the particular talents of the individual members become like the little stones that form a great mosaic. The fact that a little gold, blue, or red piece is part of a splendid mosaic makes it not less but more valuable because it contributes to an image much greater than itself. Thus, our dominant feeling toward each other can shift from jealousy to gratitude. With increasing clarity, we can see the beauty in each other and call it forth so that it may become a part of our total life together.

Both sameness and uniqueness can be affirmed in community. When we unmask the illusion that a person is the difference she or he makes, we can come together on the basis of our common human brokenness and our common need for healing. Then we also can come to the marvelous realization that hidden in the ground on which we walk together are the talents that we can offer to each other. Community, as a new way of being together, leads to the discovery or rediscovery of each other's hidden talents and makes us realize our own unique contribution to the common life.

Henri J. M. Nouwen (1932–1996), a Dutch Catholic priest, was a psychologist, writer, and member of L'Arche.

Unity

CHIARA LUBICH

I f we are united, Jesus is among us. And this has value. It is worth more than any other treasure that our heart may possess, more than mother, father, brothers, sisters, children. It is worth more than our house, our work, or our property; more than the works of art in a great city like Rome; more than our business deals; more than nature which surrounds us with flowers and fields, the sea and the stars; more than our own soul.

> ## If we are united, Jesus is among us.

It is Jesus who, inspiring his saints with his eternal truths, leaves his mark upon every age. This too is his hour. Not so much the hour of a saint but of him, of him among us, of him living in us as we build up – in the unity of love – his mystical body, the Christian community.

But we must enlarge Christ, make him grow in other members, become like him bearers of fire. Make one of all and in all, the One. It is then that we live the life that he gives us, moment by moment, in charity.

The basic commandment is brotherly love. Everything is of value if it expresses sincere fraternal charity. Nothing we do is of value if there is not the feeling of love for our brothers and sisters in it. For God is a father, and in his heart he has always and only his children.

However many neighbors you meet throughout your day, from morning to night, in all of them see Jesus. If your eye is simple, the one who looks through it is God. God is love, and love seeks to unite by winning over.

How many people, in error, look at creatures and things in order to possess them! It may be a look of selfishness or of envy, but whatever the case, it is one of sin. Or people may look within their own selves, and be possessive of their own souls, their faces lifeless because they are bored or worried. The soul, because it is an image of God, is love, and love that turns in on itself is like a flame that, because it is not fed, dies out. . . .

Out of love for Jesus, let your neighbors possess you. Like another Eucharist, let yourself "be eaten" by your neighbors. Put your entire self at their service, which is service to God, and your neighbors will come to you and love you. The fulfillment of God's every desire lies in fraternal love, which is found in his commandment: "I give you a new commandment, that you love one another" (John 13:34). ✎

Chiara Lubich (1920-2008) was an Italian religious leader, writer, and founder of the Focolare Movement.

Repentance

JOHANN CHRISTOPH ARNOLD

To forgive on a personal basis is one thing; for a fellowship to pronounce forgiveness is quite another. Is it even necessary? Granted, in many instances a wrong committed can be put right by a simple apology. In community this should be a daily experience. But grave sins may need to be brought before the community or at least before a small group of trustworthy brothers and sisters. To use the New Testament analogy of the church as a body, it would be unthinkable for an injury to one part to go unnoticed by the whole: the defenses of the entire body are mustered. So too the sin of one person in a church will affect every member.

As Stanley Hauerwas writes, "A community cannot afford to 'overlook' one another's sins because they have learned that sins are a threat to being a community of peace." Members of a united community will "no longer regard their lives as their own" or harbor their grievances as merely theirs. "When we think our brother or sister has sinned against us, such an affront is not just against us but against the whole community."

Most churches today shy away from practicing discipline. Unfortunately, because of this, members who stumble and fall have little chance for repentance, let alone a new beginning. Mark and Debbie, members of the community I belong to, experienced this firsthand before coming to join us:

"Over the years we witnessed the disastrous results of ignoring sin or secretly hiding it. We lived in a small urban community with several people, one of whom was a single man who had fallen in love with a married woman in our group. Some of us tried to tackle their affair by talking with them separately about it. Yet there was no way to really bring it out in the open – we had no mutual understanding or covenant, and no grasp of the authority Jesus had given to his church to

> **Without discipline in the community, there is no way to experience clarity or victory.**

Johann Christoph Arnold, born in 1940, is a writer and senior pastor of the Bruderhof communities.

expose and rid itself of sin – and so there was no way to experience clarity or victory.

"Under the excuse that church discipline was too harsh or fundamentalistic, too legalistic, and too judgmental, we opted for the lie that this sin wasn't a very serious matter, at least not serious enough to bring it out into the open. Didn't we all sin? Who were we to judge? Anyway, as the modern myth goes, we thought that what people needed most was loving acceptance and space to fail, not confrontation. We were under the illusion that confrontation not only added to the pain of personal shame and self-condemnation but perpetuated the cycle of failure. So we avoided it like the plague. Now we see that it was our so-called compassion that did the perpetuating.

"Tragically, the man eventually left. Two years later the woman also left the community – and divorced her husband."

Naturally I cannot advise others on how – or even whether – to practice church discipline. There is some guidance in the New Testament (e.g., 1 Cor. 5), but every situation calls for discernment. Clearly, we must reject the practice of "shunning," which is used in some denominations to separate the "righteous" from the "evildoer"; the emphasis on punishment rather than hope for redemption and reconciliation has devastating consequences.

A great deal depends on the level of commitment and accountability a community has. In a united church community whose members are accountable and committed to one another, discipline is a great gift: in rooting out sin, it can bring clarity to the most clouded situations; and by restoring those who fall, it can cleanse and enliven the body by purifying its members and giving them new faith and joy.

There are, I feel, a few basic aspects of communal discipline that must be considered if it is to be practiced redemptively. First, it must be voluntary; otherwise it will only harm the person who needs to be helped by it. Second, it must be practiced with love, sensitivity, and respect – not overzealously, not judgmentally, and certainly never with gossip. Instead of holding ourselves above the disciplined member, we need to repent with him and see where our own sin might have caused him to stumble. Our goal should never be punishment, but rather restoration.

Finally, discipline must be followed by complete forgiveness. Once the member shows himself to be repentant, he should be joyfully reaccepted, and the reason for his discipline should never be mentioned again. There are few joys as great as accepting a brother or sister who has undergone discipline back into the life of the fellowship. Repentance is a gift which we should actually all ask for again and again. ⤳

> Our goal should never be punishment, but rather restoration.

At Table

LEONARDO BOFF

Photograph by Noel Williams

Table fellowship means eating and drinking together around the same table. This is one of the most ancient signs of human intimacy, since the relationships that sustain the family are built and rebuilt continuously through it.

The table, before being a piece of furniture, marks an existential experience and a rite. It is the foremost place of the family, of communion and kinship. Meals are shared; there is the joy of gathering, of well-being without pretense, and of direct communion, which translates into uncensored commentary on daily activities and local, national, and international news.

A meal is more than just something material. It is the sacrament of reunion and communion. The food is appreciated and is the object of praise. The greatest joy of the cook is to note the satisfaction of the diners.

But we should recognize that the table is also a place of tensions and conflicts, where matters are debated openly, where differences are spelled out and agreements can be established, where disturbing silences also exist that reveal a collective malaise. Contemporary culture has so changed the sense of daily time as a result of work and productivity that it has weakened the symbolic sense of the table. This has been set aside for Sundays or special moments such as birthdays or anniversaries when family members and friends get together. But, as a general rule, it has ceased to be the fixed point of convergence of the family. Unfortunately, the table has been substituted by fast food, a quick meal that makes nutrition possible but not table fellowship.

Table fellowship is so crucial that it is linked to the very essence of the human being as human. . . . Ethno-biologists and archeologists call our attention to an interesting fact: when our anthropoid ancestors went out to gather fruit and seeds, to hunt and to fish, they did not eat individually what they were able to collect. They took the food and brought it to the group. And thus they practiced table fellowship – distributing the food among themselves and eating as a group.

Therefore, table fellowship, which assumes solidarity and cooperation with one another, enabled the first leap from animality to humanity. It was only a beginning step, but a decisive one, because it initiated a basic characteristic of the human species that sets it apart from most other species – table fellowship, solidarity, and cooperation in the act of eating. And that small distinction makes all the difference.

That table fellowship that made us human yesterday continues to renew us as human beings today. Therefore it is important to set aside time for the meal in its full meaning of table fellowship and free and disinterested conversation. It is one of the permanent sources of renewal for today's anemic humanity.

Leonardo Boff, born in 1938, is a Brazilian priest, activist, and liberation theologian.

From Property

Wassily Kandinsky, *The Ludwigskirche in Munich,* oil on cardboard (1908), Museo Thyssen-Bornemisza, Madrid

EBERHARD ARNOLD

From property to community: that is the great theme that occupies us today. First of all, we will examine the poison that lies at the root of property. Property means disintegration: it fragments the world into "mine" and "thine."

But since disintegration is decomposition, the consequence of property must be death. When our body falls apart, it decays; in the same way, when the community of humankind disintegrates into isolated individuals, each with his or her own property, it is in a state of corruption. The separation of the isolated individual is the poisonous root of property. Its curse consists in the fact that individuals no longer are connected to one another. They no longer live with each other and for each other, but only next to each other. Worst of all, individuals lose their connection to God, who is the root of all being and life. The effects are mortal.

Humankind lies in agony; it is on the brink of death. And the most obvious symptom of its deathly state is property, the outgrowth of the egoistic will to possess.

In what follows, we will explore how and why this is so. Then we will turn to search for the way out.

to Community

Let us compare humankind

to the human body, which is a God-given image of how humankind is intended to function cooperatively. When one member of the body becomes detached from the body's unity of consciousness and acts contrary to the functional unity of the whole, we recognize it as something demonic. Jesus says: "If your right hand causes you to sin, if it leads you to death, cut if off and throw it away."

1 Cor. 12:12–31

Matt. 5:30

So long as a person has unity of consciousness, all of his body's members and functions serve the unity of the whole; no member serves itself without regard for the others. But if one organ becomes independent and separates itself from the harmonious functioning of all the others, it is diseased. Likewise, when one function attracts attention to itself, disease has already supplanted health. Our heart is only in good condition so long as we do not notice it.

The same principle holds true for people. When an individual makes himself conspicuous, gives himself airs, and pushes himself forward, it is an indication of decline, indeed, of disease. The only way to avoid this fate is when each one is there for all and when all are there, in unity, for each one.

This has obvious relevance to the question of property. In fact, property – private possessions – is the root of murder. From property come war, competition, and the mutual injuriousness of business life. Property nourishes the most morbid forms of sexuality, prostitution and marriage for money (which is the same thing). And property gives birth to the lie, both in commercial dealings and in social relationships.

1 Tim. 6:9–10

James 4:1–4

I recall how some of my relatives lost a considerable sum of money in their tropical timber business. When they gathered for a family council, the question was: "How can we cut down our expenses? We cannot stop traveling first class or give up our

Eberhard Arnold, *right,* with fellow members of the first Bruderhof community in Sannerz, Germany (1920s)

In November 1929, *the Tolstoy Club in Vienna invited Eberhard Arnold, the German Protestant theologian and founder of the Bruderhof community, to hold a series of lectures. These talks, compiled in the essay above, respond to a precarious moment: both Germany and Austria, still reeling from losing the First World War, were increasingly riven by conflicts between rich and poor and extremists on the left and right. What does the gospel say in the face of such a social and religious crisis? Arnold's words continue to provoke, but with a purpose: to help us read the Old and New Testaments with more faithful eyes.*

carriage and horses, since that would damage our credit. So we can only impose restrictions in the daily life of our immediate family circle. To the outside world, we must lie – that is, we must feign wealth."

Similarly, when we go through a city we see elegantly dressed people in fine boots and expensive clothes; often these same persons live in run-down apartments or attics. Further examples are unnecessary to show how such dishonesties feed off private property; without it, they would be rendered quite harmless.

Max Stirner's book *The Individual and His Property* may well be intended as an ironic statement, though we cannot now explore to what extent this is so.[1] Be that as it may, in this book Stirner had the audacity to present the whole of modern life as consisting of nothing more than naked egoism: "Everything that I do, I do for myself."

For Stirner, this principle of egoism applies even to the love between husband and wife: such "love," he contends, is nothing more than the possessive grasping of another's body. Likewise, the friendly gestures that we offer here and there to our fellow human beings are merely the result of egoism: we are friendly to others only in order to gain possible advantages for ourselves or to extend our sphere of influence. All my acts of altruism are done only to increase my own prestige.

The logical consequence of Stirner's claim – which he openly states – is that we must recognize property as the visible extension of egoism in the material world. Thus, according to Stirner, if we want to give our children an education that will enable them to come up in the world, the central lesson we must impress on them is respect for property. Egoism and property are so completely identical that property is nothing other than the outward manifestation of egoism.

Here some will object: "Human beings, like all other living things, have received from nature, indeed from God, the instinct of self-preservation. This has been an essential force for human existence, as far back into history as we can see. If one has reverence for creation, one must recognize the instinct of self-preservation and foster it. This instinct strives after property, and rightly seeks to acquire and hold on to it. Man must live; that is his moral obligation."

This argument bears exploring. The instinct of self-preservation takes a number of forms. Biologically, it is connected to the sexual instinct: hunger and love! In politics, it comes to expression as the urge for power. In economic life, it takes form as the profit motive.

Our entire economy, in fact, is based on greed for profit: it speculates on the egoism of self-preservation and on the desire for increased power in the life of the individual. In this it has been successful. Jesus said: "If the kingdom of Satan were divided against itself, it would have long ago come to ruin." That is why, because of the unspoken agreement of all who are involved (and of all those who would like to be involved, if only they could), our highly capitalistic

Matt. 12:25–26

---

1. Max Stirner (1806–1856) published *Der Einzige und sein Eigentum* in 1844; it advocated an amoral anarchism.

From property comes war, competition, and the mutual injuriousness of business life.

Wassily Kandinsky, *Murnau, Lower Market Street,* oil on board (1908), private collection

system does not fall to pieces. The demonic forces of profit-seeking are united among themselves, pursuing the same course even when seeming to compete with each other in the marketplace.[2] So then those who possess are possessed: demonically possessed. Property, money, and the economic system have become laws unto themselves just as in the case of disorders in which the sexual function has broken out of the harmony of the body's organs and become a law unto itself. Such autonomy is demonic.

It is the curse of the present century that we bow our knees before the idol of autonomy, especially the autonomy of money and of the economic system. Western civilization is heading rapidly downhill. In the Middle Ages the church was dominant over the state and over everyday life. Later, in the age of absolutism, the state dominated the church, the economy, and daily living. Today we stand in a period of development in which the economic system dominates state,

2. Arnold's view of the "demonic" forces active in economic life is based on his reading of Matt. 6:24 ("You cannot serve God and Mammon"). As he writes in his 1915 essay "God and Mammon": "*Mamona* was the Aramaic word for wealth; and it was behind this wealth that Jesus saw the true power of Satan. The latter had said even to Jesus himself, 'I will give you all this if you will fall down and adore me.' We cannot devote ourselves to a life of outward ease and pleasure without the value we assign to these outward things becoming the predominating force in our lives. All service of Mammon contains within it a kind of reverence or secret worship of these things, a clinging to them and a love for them that denotes a decision against God. . . . Already in the early Christian period, some scholars (e.g., Gregory of Nyssa, who died after AD 394) interpreted Mammon as a name of the devil Beelzebub. Others (including Nicholas of Lyra, ca. 1300) interpreted it as the name of a demon particularly connected with money in Satan's realm." From *Salt and Light* (Plough, 1967), 76–77.

church, school, and all existence. I do not want to make a judgment here as to which is the better of these possibilities; I only want to observe that we have now arrived at a time of slavery to material things.

We have discussed the urge to self-preservation as the first counterargument to my thesis. Now we will address the second counter-argument, that of collective egoism. People make the claim: "I do not live for myself at all. I don't want to keep my property for myself; I want it for my wife and children, or for somebody else. If I go to war, I do not want to defend my own property at all – I am only doing it for the sake of all the others."

But this "for others" is really a delusion. Our extended ego is included in everything we do "for others." Marriage can easily be nothing more than egoism à deux. Those who love their spouses and children, after all, love their own flesh and blood. It's not only love to one's own family that can be a form of collective egoism. So can the solidarity of the clan, the mutual loyalty of a tribe or of pioneers in a settlement, and the common defense of an ethnicity, of a state, or, even more, of one's own caste or class in a civil war.

In determining whether apparently unselfish actions are really collective egoism, it is not the number of people whom I help that counts, but rather the nature of my help. In other words, it does not depend on whether I am looking after only myself or also those bound together with me; that is a merely arithmetical distinction. Instead, the question is whether I care *exclusively* for myself and those who belong to me, in contrast to all others.

I will say openly: I am an opponent of nationalism and patriotism. I am an opponent of the proletarian class struggle. I am an opponent of the privileges of the ownership class. I am an opponent of the political party system. What is more, I am an opponent of the right of inheritance. I maintain that egoism is to be found wherever a smaller or larger group is defending its common interests.

Our whole public life has fallen prey to the curse of property. What is the military there for? Why does the court system exist? Without a doubt, for the sake of property – something that is detached, isolated, and doomed to death.

We must burst through this atmosphere of decline and downfall. As long as what guides us is the covetous will, the fight for survival, and our personal claims and rights – as long as privileges still exist – we are lost. Then we have succumbed to a state of fragmentation and fallen away from God.

Let me give a small example: When my wife and I used to live in Berlin we learned of a woman who was badly infected with tuberculosis. She lived in a room that got no light the whole day, and she could no longer even stand up by herself. Every day one of the other occupants of the house lifted her out of bed and put her to bed again in the evening. We succeeded, after tremendous effort and by putting together all our funds, in renting a sunny room for her in

The curse of our age is that we bow our knees before the idol of autonomy.

Wassily Kandinsky,
Landscape with Chimneys,
oil on canvas (1910),
Solomon R. Guggenheim
Museum, New York

a healthy district. And when we came to fetch her, she refused to leave her old room for the new one; she had become so accustomed to her appalling surroundings. Isn't this incredible?

But let us examine ourselves. Are we any different? We have grown accustomed to the curse of property, of isolation, of a fragmented life. We must wake up and hear the gospel which will make us free from the curse of a life without the Spirit and without God.

Let us turn our gaze to nature in order to recover from these shocking pictures. From a purely natural point of view, what does life consist of? We live from the sun, the air, water, and the treasures of the soil. We live by our own working strength, utilizing these forces of nature through the exertion of our body and spirit. To whom is the sun given? It is given to all – to everyone without exception. If there is anything that people do have in common, it is the gift of the sun. (To be sure, there are people who live a shadowy existence, but they would do well to come out into the sunlight!)

The sixteenth-century Hutterites say in their writings: If the sun were not hung so high, people would long ago have claimed it as their own – to the detriment of everyone else, who would no longer be able to see it. The will to possess, to take for yourself things that do not belong to you, would not even stop at the sun. Fortunately, though, the sun is hung up too high![3]

What about the air? In part, it is already bought and sold. Don't health resorts charge for their good air? Even so, the air does not belong to them. What about

3. Peter Walpot, *Das grosse Artikelbuch,* Neumühl, Moravia, 1577, in *Glaubenszeugnisse oberdeutscher Taufgesinnter,* Bd.2, ed. Robert Friedmann, (Gütersloh, 1967), 231ff.

water? Isn't it already treated as a commodity? And the earth? Is there reasonable ground for dividing up the earth as personal property – is it any different from the sun? No! The earth should not be private property either. The earth belongs to the inhabitants of the earth, to those for whom God ordained it. *Lev. 25:23*

But today the earth is to be found in "private" hands. What, in fact, does *private* mean? We speak of private affairs, private roads, private property, and so forth. *Privare* is Latin, and it means: *to rob*. Private property is stolen property.[4] From whom is it robbed? It is robbed from God and from humankind. It is pilfered from God's creation and appropriated by individuals – or inherited by them, which in principle is the same thing. Naturally, whoever inherits or acquires property also holds on to it tightly.

While these examples from the world of nature clearly illustrate the curse of property, nevertheless people need prophetic voices to lay it clearly before their eyes. God has sent such prophets again and again.

Jesus is the friend of man – and therefore he is the enemy of property. In other words, just because Jesus wants true life for humankind, therefore he is the enemy of the instinct of self-preservation, of an egotistical existence. According to one of Paul's letters, every person is to be of like mind as Jesus. Jesus did not *Phil. 2:1–11* hold on to his privileges, but gave up everything and held on to nothing, taking the lowest place in society. He was not only the poorest of all – he was even classed as a criminal. He held on to nothing for himself, including money; his *John 12:6* itinerant community had a communal purse. He taught: Whoever lives for the *John 12:25* sake of preserving his own life has lost his life, and whoever wants to keep his life must lose it. Anyone who does not forsake all that he has is not of me. *Luke 14:33*

No one is of Jesus who still holds on to his property. Jesus tells us: Sell all that *Luke 18:18–25* you have and give it away. Whoever has more than one coat should give it away. You should also give your second hour of work – that part of your labor that *Matt. 5:40–42* gives rise to surplus and thus becomes the source of property. Someday, when all goods, just like the sun and the earth, belong to the common weal – that is, to God and his kingdom – then your second hour of work will also belong to God and to all humankind. Gain a fortune, but not here where moth and rust can *Luke 12:33* destroy it – gather it up in heaven! Free yourselves from all rights and privileges!

Until now we have spoken only of property, of what we want to turn *away from*, but now we will speak of community, the goal that we want to turn *toward*. For giving up our property can only mean one thing: dedicating ourselves to community with all we have and are.

It was Nietzsche who said that Jesus contrasts a real life with a false one.[5]

---

4. Pierre-Joseph Proudhon, *What is Property? An Inquiry into the Principle of Right and of Government* (1840), chapter 3 §1.
5. See Friedrich Nietzsche, *Sämtliche Werke: Kritische Studienausgabe in 15 Bänden*, vol.13, ed. Giorgio Colli and Mazzino Montinari (de Gruyter, 1980), 106.

Our life in all its aspects must be a symbol of the coming kingdom of God.

What is the true life that we should lead – what does it mean to be alive? A body is alive when all the organs and functions work together in unity for one another and for the tasks of the body. Life exists where there is a cohesive, dynamic *unity:* unity of movement, unity in multiplicity, unity in consciousness, unity in will, in feeling, and in thought. Life is organic unity.

Likewise, an individual is only fully alive insofar as he or she is part of a united humanity. And humanity is united only insofar as it is led and determined by one collective soul, by one spirit of community in which all stand up for all and all work for all.

If we want community, we must want the *spirit* of community. That is why I reject the so-called communist form of community. I believe only in that community which believes in the Spirit: the community whose collective soul is the Holy Spirit. In the Spirit, the church is unanimous and united; in the Spirit, the church is rich in gifts and powers and various expressions.

But just as in the body, unity can only be maintained through sacrifice, so also in the church community, unity can only be maintained through sacrifice. As we have already seen, if this unity were to be achieved without sacrifice then it would only be the gratification of a form of collective selfishness. In the church, however, each individual must be ready to sacrifice all his strength, yes, even to

John 15:13

surrender his life. Only one who is ready to give up his life for his brothers and sisters truly loves. If we want to set our hands to work in church community – if we want to enter into the church and belong to the Spirit that animates it – then our hands must first let go of all else and be open and free for service.

If we can comprehend this mystery, then we will understand that this way is *life-affirming*. It is not a matter of dying for the sake of dying, but of letting go for the sake of a rebirth. It means turning away from illusions in order to win reality, renouncing inessentials in order to attain essentials. What will come over this world is fire, a network of holy torches, a network of organic, living cells.

The early Christians were in the habit of speaking unphilosophically and simply. In order to illustrate the coming future of humankind, they used two pic-

Matt. 22:1–14; 25:1–13
Rev. 19:6–7
Eph. 5:31–32

tures: the table and the wedding feast. All people shall be united in the kingdom like a gathering around one table; all shall be united as in one wedding party. The unity between one man and one woman in marriage is to be the symbol of the unity between God and his people.

This is our task in church community. It consists in making our whole life in all its aspects a symbol of the future of humankind in the coming kingdom of God. And so: away from property, onward to community! ➷

Translated from German by Kathleen Hasenberg and Emmy Barth Maendel based on Eberhard Arnold's lecture notes. Footnotes and scripture references have been added by the editors.

Rainfall

1.

The rain enchants me with all its wild, foolish worship,
days when it is difficult to pray.
God is out there, up there, men say –
up there, or not at all: Heaven is a place
with a postbox, whose address we have lost.

But to regard the rainfall –
there is a pattern for our prayer:
no Anglo-Saxon philanthropy
pledging help from its place, staying separate
from the slimy ditch, remaining sky-bound;

but each bead breaks off, is lost from its kind,
and descending, seeks the hollow deep,
mixing with low earthen things, becoming mud.

A young man came to Abba Sisoes, saying,
I see in myself that the remembrance of God
remains with me. But the elder replied,

It is no great thing that your thought should be with God.
But it is a great thing to consider yourself
lower than the whole of his creation.

2.

Praise to the Maker of the torrent
and the hurricane,
praise for the fierce humility of rain:

whose motion will not end, neither come to rest
nor ascend again until, like grace,
it finds the lowest empty place.

MATTHEW BAKER

Why Community

America's most frequently quoted theologian talks with Plough
editor Peter Mommsen about the Benedict Option, evangelism,
marriage, Christian communism, and why voting is overrated.

AN INTERVIEW WITH STANLEY HAUERWAS

Peter Mommsen: *Stanley, if I could sum up
your influential career as a writer, you aim to
help people live out the gospel more fully. Is that
a fair description?*

Stanley Hauerwas: I certainly hope so. I try
to call attention to people who are living out
the gospel in a way that makes my own life

but a very pale reflection. I am thinking of
people like Jean Vanier, the founder of the
L'Arche community. If I know of anyone who
is genuinely holy, it is Jean Vanier – not that
he would ever think of himself that way. So in
my writing about how to live according to the
gospel, how to live to *become* the gospel, I try

Is Dangerous

to direct attention to real people, not just to beliefs or concepts.

You've written extensively about how the church should respond to the "end of Christendom" – the fact that we no longer live in a culture whose ground rules stem from Christianity. What about the "Benedict Option" proposed by the writer Rod Dreher? He argues that Christians should respond to secularization by following the example of the early monastics, withdrawing from a heathen civilization to build alternative communities where Christian virtues can be nourished and passed on. Is he right?

This Benedict Option idea comes from the last line of Alasdair MacIntyre's book *After Virtue*, in which he observes that the barbarians have been ruling us for some time and that our future is "no doubt to have a Benedict, no doubt a very different Benedict." Here's the problem: Alasdair once told me that this is the

---

Stanley Hauerwas, professor emeritus of theological ethics and of law at Duke University, is author or editor of more than thirty books including (with William H. Willimon) Resident Aliens: Life in the Christian Colony *(Abingdon, 1989, 2014). Watch this interview at* plough.com/hauerwas.

line he most regrets ever having written! He wasn't advocating some kind of withdrawal strategy – he was only pointing out that we can't be compromised by the world in which we find ourselves. I don't think your community, the Bruderhof, takes a withdrawal strategy, for instance.

I sometimes say that I wouldn't mind withdrawing, but we're surrounded – there's no place to withdraw to! Maybe the Benedict Option should be rethought in terms of the vow of stability and what it might look like in congregations. We would tell prospective members: "When you join our church, you don't get to decide by yourself when and where you will move. If your company wants to send you to a new town, you first need to ask the church whether it's a good idea."

For Christians, to be nonviolent means always being open to having the violence of our lives exposed.

That kind of accountability to one another is only possible in a community where there is mutual commitment – where there is a church discipline.

Right. My hunch is that you don't just make a community up. You discover that you need one another because you're in danger. We need to figure out how to reclaim the disciplines that are necessary for building a communal life in a manner that indicates that we are a people who need help. We need to pray to God to help us, because we're not quite sure anymore where we are – we're not quite sure what the dangers are. We need all the help we can get from one another, and we need God in order to know how to be accountable to one another.

What do you mean that we can't just make community up?

First, community for community's sake is not a good idea. Sartre is right: hell is other people! Community by itself cannot overwhelm the loneliness of our lives. I think we are a culture that produces extreme loneliness. Loneliness creates a hunger – and hunger is the right word, indicating as it does the physical character of the desire and need to touch another human being.

But such desperate loneliness is very dangerous. Look at NFL football. Suddenly you're in a stadium with a hundred thousand people and they are jumping up and down. Their bodies are painted red, like the bodies that surround them. They now think their loneliness has been overcome. I used to give a lecture in my basic Christian Ethics class that I called "The Fascism of College Basketball." You take alienated upper-middle-class kids who are extremely unsure of who they are – and suddenly they are Duke Basketball. I call it Duke Basketball Fascism because fascism has a deep commitment to turning the modern nation-state into a community. But to make the modern state into a kind of community – for the state to become the primary source of identity through loose talk about community – is very dangerous. It is not community for its own sake that we seek. Rather, we should try to be a definite *kind* of community.

Alasdair MacIntyre, for one, resists being called a communitarian – he fears that in this place and time such calls are bound to lead to nationalistic movements. Those who hunger for community should never forget Nuremberg.

In confronting Nazism in the 1930s, Eberhard Arnold, the founder of the Bruderhof communities, used to repeat that our goal must never be community, only Jesus.

What I admire about Arnold is his Christ-centered vision. In some ways I think of Eberhard Arnold as an early Barth. He recovered the centrality of Jesus in a way that was extraordinarily impressive.

I think that his stress on how you need one another to know who Christ is was one of the great gifts of the Anabaptists. In many ways, the left wing of the Reformation was the Catholic reformers, not Protestant reformers. So I find in Arnold a commitment to a view of the church that seems to me very Catholic, at least in the sense that he emphasizes that the church must take material form. He insists that there must be a living, visible body of believers.

War, Peace, and Evangelism

For Arnold, as for the sixteenth-century Anabaptists, faithfulness to Jesus meant nonviolence – going the way of the defenseless Christ. Should nonviolence be part of the church's communal discipline?

Well, it's important first of all to distinguish between Christian-community nonviolence and nonviolence qua nonviolence. The problem with the word *nonviolence* is that people think they know what nonviolence is *apart from Christ*. Then nonviolence becomes a marker more determinative than Jesus – it conceives peace apart from the crucifixion. But in reality, *discipleship* is the defining characteristic of what it means for Christians to be nonviolent. It means always being open to having the violence of our lives exposed.

Talking about nonviolence presupposes you've got to know what violence is in order to know the "non." I don't like the language of pacifism either because it's so passive. What I like to talk about is peace, and peace is hard

work in which oftentimes conflict is required. It involves acknowledging the violence we often misidentify as peace. What's important is how a community becomes shaped by Christ in such a way that we are able to reject the falsehoods that lead us to use coercion.

You've insisted that "it is not the task of the church to ensure a stable world" (The Work of Theology, 69). *What then is the church's response when confronted with the atrocities of ISIS, including the wholesale slaughter of fellow Christians? The Archbishop of Mosul, for one, has been calling for the international community to defend the innocent, if necessary with military force.*

I don't know how to answer those kinds of questions. One of the failures that such questions elicit is our lack of any sense of Christian unity. What happened to Iraqi Christians is absolutely horrendous. The fact that Christians in America didn't feel or didn't care about what was going on there was a failure to acknowledge our Christian unity.

What would unity have meant? Well, it might have meant sending missionaries to be present in Iraq. That might have offered some protection, because it's easier to kill Iraqis with impunity than to kill Americans.

Still, if you ask, "Stanley, what is your foreign policy toward ISIS?", I don't have one. But I do maintain that love to our persecuted brothers and sisters must mean facing the same dangers that they are undergoing. That's why I'm a big fan of the Christian Peacemaker Teams. For instance, they'll go to Hebron where Jewish soldiers and Palestinian activists are toe to toe, ready to kill one another. The Christian Peacemaker Team will come in and say, "Can we fix you guys a meal?" It doesn't sound like much, but eating together is a big deal. It's a start.

If the church's task is not to ensure social stability, then what is it? You've famously described the church as a colony. We were just speaking of Eberhard Arnold, who used a similar image: that of the embassy, based on Paul's words that "we are ambassadors for Christ" (2 Cor. 5:20). He wrote in 1934: "In the residence of the ambassador, only the laws of the country he represents are valid. We are ambassadors of the kingdom of God. This means that we do nothing at all except what the king of God's kingdom would himself do for his kingdom." What's your take?

The church doesn't have a mission. The church *is* mission.

I like this. I have high regard for ambassadors in the State Department because they are, in a certain way, hostages we sent out, having to negotiate a world in which they are not in control. I understand they're surrounded by Marines and so on. Nevertheless, we send them out to be peaceful representatives of the United States, and oftentimes by having to learn to live in a foreign country they become sympathetic with the people they're coming to know, people who are different from ourselves. In this way they come back and teach us what these folks are about in a way that helps us not to demonize them.

So Arnold's words touch on a very interesting way to think about mission. We could put it this way: as Christians, we are establishing embassies around the world in which some of our brothers and sisters are being held hostage – so that we might learn better who the folks are that we want to tell about Jesus.

And that's the church's mission?

The church doesn't have a mission. The church *is* mission. Our fundamental being is based on the presumption that we are witnesses to a Christ who is known only through witnesses. To be a witness means you bear the marks of Christ so that your life gives life to others. I can't imagine Christians who are not fundamentally in mission as constitutive of their very being – because you don't know who Christ is except by someone else telling you who Christ is. That's the work of the Holy Spirit.

Therefore it is the task of Christians to embody the joy that comes from being made part of the body of Christ. That joy should be infectious and pull other people toward it. How many of us have actually asked another person to follow Christ? In my experience, far too few.

Politics and Marriage

What is the church's witness in the public square in an election year? Should Christians be organizing politically? Should we be voting?

I think voting is way overvalued. One, you forget that voting is a coercive activity. It's where 50.1 percent get to tell 49.9 percent what to do. People forget that voting is not supposed to be an end in itself. Instead, it is a means to force conversation between people that otherwise would not happen. And that's great. Of course I take it that at the Bruderhof and other intentional communities the majority doesn't win – I mean, you've got to talk it out.

That's right, there's no majority rule, at least if we're living as we should be, and no minority rule either. Our aim is to make decisions unanimously. That's why we pray for the Holy Spirit.

Exactly. And that means that oftentimes, given the divisions within the community, you simply can't make a decision. You have to be patient.

Democracy in its fundamental form is also patience. It requires you to listen, in the Pauline sense, to the lesser member, and sometimes, if the lesser member isn't convinced, you have to wait.

Looming behind this year's presidential campaign are, of course, the September 11 attacks. That trauma continues to be operative in American politics. Our nation, allegedly the strongest in the world, runs on fear. The American people are frightened to death.

Fear, by the way, is the reason that our foreign policy is just the flip side of our commitment to developing increasingly technological forms of medicine. We hope that medical technology will get us out of life alive! The American people simply don't seem to know how to deal with death – we're basically a death-denial country.

Denial of death might be why there now seems to be a concerted campaign for the acceptance of euthanasia. We seek to disguise the reality of disease and dying with the illusion that we're in control.

Yes. I say that in a hundred years, if Christians are identified as people who do not kill their children or the elderly, we will have done well. Because that's clearly coming.

Does electoral politics have a place in combatting evils like these?

Sure. Christians can run for office. I just want them to run as Christians. They may even be elected once – you never know! But how to speak the truth in the public arena as a Christian is a deep challenge.

Speaking the truth in the Christian arena can be a big challenge too. Take same-sex marriage, which continues to split churches across the denominational spectrum – as someone who attends an Episcopalian church, you've seen this firsthand. How do we learn to speak the truth to each other about marriage, about singleness, about sexuality?

The first thing we need to say is that we want to make marriage difficult for people to enact. The idea that falling in love is sufficient for getting married is just a deep bedevilment. In order for two people to be married and have their marriage witnessed by the church, we need to know how their marriage is going to build up the holiness of the community. In practice, this means they may not be terribly attracted to one another. We forget that for centuries Christians married one another and had sex on their wedding night even though they didn't know one another; they may well have never met one another until the day of the wedding. And yet the church blessed it because the community would hold them to the promises they had made. That's why divorce and remarriage is such a serious issue.

So marriage is not something to be done because two people think they love one another. Rather it's based on faithfulness to one another in the community such that over a lifetime, we're able to look back on the relationship and call it love. Faithfulness becomes the defining mark of Christian marriage.

And how do you define marriage?

Well, I don't define it but I will describe it. Marriage is the lifelong commitment to be

> **If in a hundred years Christians are identified as people who do not kill their children or the elderly, we will have done well.**

Image from www.scrowing.org

faithful to one another, not only in terms of sexual relations but in terms of being attentive to your first responsibility to the person to whom you have pledged your life. Marriage gives witness to the same kind of faithfulness of Christ to his church. Part of this commitment includes hospitality to new life, which results from sexual relations.

That is the sticking point I have toward gay marriage. Not every marriage between a man and a woman is necessarily procreative. But marriage as an institution of the church of Jesus Christ is only intelligible in terms of the Christian willingness to have a child.

Community of Goods

Now that we've covered politics and marriage, let's talk about money – specifically, community of goods. What is the relevance of Acts 2 and 4 for the church today?

I don't know that the Bruderhof mode of communal sharing is the only way to go.

Neither do we.

Right. But there's something to it. Years ago I was giving a lecture at Houston Baptist University at their new business school. At the dinner before the lecture, the associate dean of the school told me how her church grew between fifty and one hundred members every Sunday. My lecture was called "Why Business Ethics Is a Bad Idea." When I finished the lecture, the dean said, "This just sounds so despairing. Isn't there something we can do?" I said, "Yes, but it's too late for your students. By the time they get to business school they're too corrupt. However, I think before you let anyone join your church you ought to have them disclose how much they make. 'I make $85,000 a year. I want to be a member of the church.' 'I make $150,000, I want to be a member.'" She said, "Well, we couldn't do that. That's private." I said, "Where are the fundamentalists when you need them? God knocked off Sapphira and Ananias for not sharing what they made. Where did all this privacy stuff come from?"

So when it comes to money, maybe we should begin by telling one another what we make. That would be a very small first step, but at least it's a way to start. For instance, at my church the rector knows approximately what I make, which as a full-time professor at Duke is about $100,000 per year. The problem that you run into is that many congregation members don't want to expose their income – not because they're making so much, but because they're

making so little, and they value their lives based on what they earn.

Money is a power. The more of it we have, the more subject we make ourselves to it.

That's a danger every Christian has to reckon with – the power of mammon. It's definitely not a danger that members of intentional community are immune to. That said, what are the gifts that Christian intentional communities can make to the wider church? And what are the dangers to avoid?

I think the danger for you in the Bruderhof is that you're too impressive: people say, "Well, *they* can live that way but not me. I can't see how we could ever live that way!" So you risk being an example that is praised but dismissed.

On the other hand, you do have a contribution to make to more conventional forms of Christianity. The reform of the church across the centuries has always come from monastics, and you're part of that movement. You're married monastics. I think we will just have to wait and see how God's going to use you to help those of us who live more conventionally. We need to better understand how the kinds of commitments you represent are necessary for the whole church.

One of those commitments is to live in such a way that the church becomes, in your words, "a visible and bodily reality." Of course, that reality isn't confined to communities like ours. Where else do you see it today?

I think it's more of a reality than we're often able to see. People always ask me, "Where's your church?" I'm an Episcopalian – I mean, you don't become more compromised than that! But at the church I attend – the Church of the Holy Family in Durham, North Carolina – we see people who appear quite ordinary, and yet show an extraordinary thoughtfulness. Right now, for instance, one member is mobilizing a number of us to support one of our former members who is dying in Florida. I believe that that is God at work; that's God showing up even in an Episcopalian church. I think God shows up many places, even among Southern Baptists! ✒

This interview from March 4, 2016 has been edited for clarity and concision.

Before you let anyone join your church, you ought to have them disclose how much they make.

Confessing to One Another

The Uncomfortable but Liberating Gift of Openness

JOHNNY FRANSHAM

"Confess your sins to one another and pray for one another, that you may be healed."

—James 5:16

Recently, a couple from our church returned home after a mission trip. They met many seeking hearts in their travels – people who felt the need to change and who wanted something new. But when they talked with people about the forgiveness Jesus offers through the confession of sins, they were met with mixed reactions: "God has already forgiven me." "Do I really have to confess my sins in order to be forgiven?" "Isn't God's grace sufficient?"

God's grace indeed abounds, but this is especially so when we unburden our lives before another person. Sin and guilt always work in secret. Dietrich Bonhoeffer writes:

> In the confession of concrete sins the old man dies a painful, shameful death before the eyes of a brother. Because this humiliation is so hard, we continually scheme to avoid it. Yet in the deep mental and physical pain of humiliation before a brother we experience our rescue and salvation.*

Confessing one's sins to someone – even someone we trust – is never easy because it means becoming vulnerable; it means admitting we need help. In a world that exalts individual achievement and despises weakness, revealing one's sins to another feels extremely uncomfortable. Then there is the fear of gossip which can so quickly circulate, especially in tight-knit Christian groups.

But all this can be an excuse, a copout for not really turning away from sin. Hiding behind our Christianity, we keep our sin secret, not because we feel forgiven but because we fear wounded pride. Self-righteousness and the desire to look good have become so entrenched in us that instead of being the sinners we are, we lock ourselves behind a spiritual façade of our own making – a prison that keeps us isolated from each other and from God.

My wife and I founded our marriage on our urge to follow Christ above all else. We have fallen short of this many times, but just as often we have experienced that by confessing our failings openly to each other we find a deeper unity and love and are able to help each other. It has become blindingly obvious to me that keeping secrets from my wife – particularly about my temptations and sins – only damages our marriage.

Isn't the same true of all our relationships? If we long for peace, unity, and love in our fellowship with one another, then we must become vulnerable and reveal what we are hiding in the dark. When the apostle Paul urges us to carry each other's burdens, he means this to lead us nearer to Jesus and, in the end, to one another. It is a gift, not a begrudging duty. The First Letter of John is as sharp as it is hopeful: "If we claim to have fellowship with him yet walk in the darkness, we lie and do not live by the truth. But if we walk in the light, as he is in the light, we have fellowship with one another."

What does it mean to walk in the light, to come clean? To truly give up what Christ wants to take away? Like the paralyzed man described in Matthew 9, we are all afflicted with some kind of sickness or infirmity. More importantly, most of us are weighed down by our sins and failures. This is why the apostle James urges us to call the elders of the church to pray, as well as to confess our sins to one another. Through confession, we can unlock the bars that keep us bound up inside. Then we find true and lasting healing. But for this to happen, we must be ready for Christ to change us. Perhaps this is why we resist confessing anything to anybody. For to admit our wrong-doings to another person would mean we are ready to change the way we are and live. Jesus promises to make everything new, but also says, "Go and sin no more" (John 8:11).

Yes, God knows everything, and we can always come directly to him. His forgiveness is a wonderful gift. But its power to free and heal comes at a cost: we must allow ourselves to be made low so that Christ himself can truly lift us up to new life.

When we confess our sins to one another, we go the lowly way of Jesus, who was born in a manger and died on a cross. We meet this Christ in our brother and sister. It is a mystery, but the humble way is the only way that leads to light and hope, freedom and joy. Then, as Jesus said, "the kingdom of God is in your midst" (Luke 17:21). ⤳

* Dietrich Bonhoeffer, *Life Together: The Classic Exploration of Christian in Community* (HarperOne, 2009), 114.

Johnny Fransham, together with his wife Anna Regula (Regi), served as bishop for the European communities of the Bruderhof from 2006–2016. On February 8 of this year, he died at age sixty-seven after a three-month battle with cancer. Read about his life at bruderhof.com/fransham.

The Way

Two Millennia of Christian Community

ALDEN BASS

he history of committed Christian community is a story of roads. The first followers of Jesus called themselves "the Way," a name that echoes Jewish *halakha,* the "way of life" enshrined in the Torah, as well as the disciples' belief that Jesus was "the way" to God the Father.

The earliest community that formed in Jerusalem after Jesus' execution was composed of the original disciples and pilgrims who had traveled to Jerusalem to celebrate the holy days. United by the conviction that Jesus' resurrection was a sign of covenant renewal and the new creation, these Jews marched through the Red Sea of baptism into a radically new way of life, one in which all possessions were held in common, there were no needy persons, and all members were "of one heart and mind." The spirit of ancient Israel engulfed the Holy City, and for a brief period of time the utopian community of the Jubilee was reconstituted.

Alden Bass is an associate professor of theology at Saint Louis University and co-founder of the Lotus House community in St. Louis, Missouri.

Eventually, war drove all the Christians and Jews from the land. Still, the traces of that original movement were so impressed in their memory that the disciples who fled Jerusalem continued to establish countercultural communities of economic sharing, scripture study, participatory worship, and service to the poor.

These first Christians wended the path pioneered by Jesus. They were not the only people to live intentionally; in the early centuries of the Common Era there were other fraternal associations of mutual aid, organized by profession, religious devotion, or simply voluntary adherence. Christian communities differed from them, as Tertullian observed in the third century, in their charity to the underserved (*Apology* 39.5–6). Groups of Christians organized themselves into economic communities called parishes, a word derived from the Greek *paroikia,* which meant "neighbor" but also "sojourner" or "pilgrim." So, just as "parish" is similar to "pariah" in English, the name would have reminded Christians they were outcasts and exiles in a foreign land.

Palestinian roads were treacherous, consisting of packed earthen pathways, usually narrow and winding around the many mountains in the region. Persecution forced whole families of Christians to follow these dusty trails to new cities, where they formed tightly knit communities of a few dozen people. In times of difficulty, Christians relied on one another for basic needs. For instance, if Christians were imprisoned, they counted on the community to bring them food and care for them. Such pressures bound the parish together into a family unit, sometimes called "the household of faith."

The development of Roman highways – between eight and thirty feet wide; built in courses of gravel, sand, and pavement; engineered to efficiently drain water away – not only made life easier but also aided the spread of Christianity throughout the empire. As external pressures relaxed, Christians' dependence on one another likewise waned. By the end of the third century, the parish had morphed from a countercultural community into an administrative jurisdiction of the institutional church. This shift occurred at different rates in different regions, but by the end of the fourth century Christianity was the official religion of the Roman Empire and firmly established in major urban areas. From this point until the modern period, Christians in Europe would live in tension between a supposedly "Christian" society and the communal ideal of the early church.

The Birth of Monasticism

 ronically, one man credited with the renewal of Christian community spent most of his life living as a hermit in the Egyptian desert. Anthony was born in 250 to an affluent family in Lower Egypt. His parents died while he was young, and Anthony received a significant inheritance. One day, entering a church just as the gospel was being read, he heard the lector say: "If anyone would be perfect, go, sell what you have, and give it to the poor, and you will have treasure in heaven; and come, follow me." Immediately Anthony sold his possessions and distributed the money to the poor. He lived as an outcast on the margins of the village, seeking God alone in the wilderness. For twenty years, he prepared the way of the Lord through prayer, fasting, and vigils. As his reputation grew, others followed him down the deserted highway into the wilderness, settling in individual cells near him. These pilgrims were called "monks," from the Greek *monos,* which means "alone."

Although Christianity was now accepted throughout the empire, some Christians

Juan Rizi,
*Saint Benedict
at Table*

the monks into communal houses under the leadership of an elder. The men ate together, held their goods in common, and followed a common order of communal prayer, manual labor, and later, bible study. Their way of life was called cenobitic, from the Greek *koinos biosi,* "common life." Within a few years, Pachomius had three thousand followers, and by the mid-fourth century there were several men's houses and, situated on the other side of the Nile, at least one house for women. After Pachomius died his followers wrote down his communal rules, which were published in Latin by Jerome and became well known, the first of many such communal covenants.

believed the faith to be weakened, diluted by its social respectability and assimilated to prevailing cultural norms. Inspired by Anthony's example to recover the original vision of Jesus' followers, many divested themselves of property and worldly concerns, leaving even the security of marriage to pursue a simple life of prayer and manual labor. For them, commitment to God was not a matter of words (they spoke few) but of action. They eschewed luxury in all forms, preferring simple food, plain dress, and basic shelter. They even surrendered their autonomy by submitting themselves to the oversight of a spiritual elder called an abbot (from *abba,* "father"). These decisions eventually evolved into the three monastic vows of poverty, chastity, and obedience.

The "way of the Lord" was soon jammed with traffic as waves of would-be monks entered the deserts of Egypt, Syria, and Palestine. The men began to join together in large colonies, meeting occasionally for prayer and communion. This common life was given form by Pachomius, who organized

At the time, most of the monks who left the city for the desert were uneducated laymen dissatisfied with the worldliness of the church. Basil of Caesarea, a well-educated nobleman from Cappadocia, was an exception. He attempted to incorporate monastic principles in an urban setting under the guidance of church leaders. He wrote his own *Rule* and established a community at his family's estate near the Black Sea. His goal was to balance the individualism and personal holiness of the desert monks with Jesus' call to engage the world with acts of justice and mercy. To that end, Basil built one of the world's first hospitals in his community, a place to offer hospitality especially to those who could not afford medical care. The hospital was an integral part of the intentional community, which was named the Basiliad after its founder. Physicians and nurses lived on the grounds, as did students studying at the attached medical school. The complex also included space to host travelers and to provide education. Basil's *Rules* remain the basis for monastic life in the Orthodox churches of Turkey, Greece, Syria, and Russia.

Until the fourth century, communal activity was concentrated in the east, but eventually all roads lead to Rome. Monastic ideals arrived by way of travelers from Egypt and Syria and through stories being published about the monks. John Cassian lived among the eastern monks for years, then wrote several influential books in Latin about what he had learned. His audience was a new generation of urban Christians forming communities in cities across Europe. Many [including a number of aristocratic Roman women,] were inspired to retread the Palestinian roads Jesus had walked. Under the guidance of Jerome, this circle of heiresses adopted a life of simplicity, common prayer, fasting, and charitable works. One of the women, Melania the Elder, moved to Jerusalem in 378 and led a community of about fifty women on the Mount of Olives. Many of these women took vows of celibacy and devoted themselves to biblical study. Another community was established at Bethlehem. Back in Italy, the bishop Ambrose formulated policies for the many young women who wanted to live out the gospel around Milan.

Like Basil, the French bishop Caesarius of Arles believed that monastic ideals should be integrated into the life of the parish church. Caesarius preached hundreds of sermons to his congregation on prayer, fasting, chastity, compassion, and social justice throughout the fifth century. He exhorted all the Christians in the twenty-five or so rural parishes of his diocese to practice mutual love and responsibility for one another – to be communities. His sermons continued to circulate for centuries after his death, inspiring generations of Christians to live out radical Christian values in their everyday lives.

Outside of the New Testament, perhaps no text has been as important to the development of Christian community as the *Rule of Benedict,* written in the early sixth century and shaped by the writings of John Cassian and the anonymously written *Rule of the Master.* Benedict, a Roman nobleman, left Rome for the countryside, where he established several monastic communities. Everyone in the community shared the responsibilities of tending the farm and the kitchen. Work was punctuated eight times each day by common prayer called "the hours." Benedict's vision for common life – which integrated work and prayer, solitude and community, personal responsibility and authority – was extraordinarily successful, and remained the paradigm for Christian communities for well over a millennium. His emphasis on stability and fidelity to a particular locality would become hallmarks of intentional Christian community.

As the roads of the crumbling empire fell into disrepair, the monasteries became isolated, scattered outposts. The monks were fantastically successful – erudite and wealthy – but they lost themselves in contemplation. The monastic life of prayer and study became professionalized and the way of simplicity and manual labor was eventually lost. Caricatures of fat monks began to appear in this period. A series of reforms in the Middle Ages struggled to recover Benedict's original vision, first the Cluniac reforms in the tenth century, then the Carthusians in the eleventh. The Cistercians likewise attempted to restore the simplicity of the original Benedictine spirit: they made time for more manual labor, stripped their chapels of rich art and décor, and adopted a simple worship style. Much later, the Trappists would re-reform the Cistercians, adding their own emphasis on silence.

EVANGELICAL COMMUNITIES OF THE MIDDLE AGES

espite these reforms, the monasteries could not contain the radical impulse of Christianity. Europe was undergoing major social and economic change during the twelfth century, moving from a feudal, village-centered society to an urban economy. The ancient cities, dormant since the time of Benedict, were awakening with new commerce. The Roman roads were cleared and rebuilt. Yet as trade increased, the division between rich and poor also widened. Alongside a rising urban middle-class of merchants, bankers, and lawyers grew an underclass of poor and underemployed. Beginning with monks such as Rupert of Deutz (who wrote a little treatise titled *On the Truly Apostolic Life*) a movement arose to restore the model of the Jerusalem community for the entire church. Others, such as Gerhoh of Reichersberg, argued that if monasticism is the pattern for the church, then all Christians should be monks of a sort: God's call to the Christian life is universal, not limited to the cloister. The apostolic life, they said, was not simply a life of prayer and devotion but of social and economic justice. Ordinary Christians should reconcile economic divisions through solidarity with the poor, banding together with those marginalized by the new economy through fraternal charity, scripture study, voluntary poverty, and active proclamation of the faith.

This awakening led to the formation of small evangelical communities across Europe. In western France, Robert d'Abrissel gathered a diverse group of men and women, including a number of former prostitutes, into a community at Fontevrault known as Christ's Poor. In southern France, groups of Christians known as the *cathari,* or "pure ones," organized radical communities that rejected sexual relations, the eating of meat, and hierarchical authority. The Cathars were regarded as heretics because of their denigration of the material creation, and were relentlessly persecuted. Northern Italy produced a movement called the *humiliati,* or "humble ones," in which both clerics and laypeople attempted to conform their lives to the gospel call to simplicity. The movement included both celibate and married people, many of whom were drawn from the thriving garment industry in the area. Though the communities produced rich cloth in the textile industry, they wore only plain, undyed clothes. They refrained from political engagement, served the disadvantaged, and prayed the Benedictine hours. By the end of the thirteenth century, there were communities of Humiliati in most cities in northern Italy.

In southern France, a wealthy merchant named Peter Waldo led a similar movement. In a story not unlike Anthony's, Waldo gave up his business, made reparation for his dishonest dealings, and began distributing bread in the streets of Lyons. Others followed his example of poverty and commitment to studying the Bible, and they became known as the Poor Men of Lyons. The "Waldensian" movement spread quickly to Germany and Italy, where it eventually merged with the Humiliati. Small communes formed which engaged in common work and gospel preaching; some remain to this day.

Saint Francis became the most famous exemplar of the apostolic life. Like so many earlier community leaders, Francis was a scion of aristocrats, who relinquished all his wealth, even the clothes on his back (he literally went naked for a time). Exchanging rich silk garb for a rough woolen habit, Francis and his friends traipsed across Europe preaching and exhorting people to follow Jesus' way. Before long the roads of medieval Europe were clogged with tens of thousands of friars singing, preaching, and begging for daily bread. The Franciscan movement spread throughout the continent, spilling over into North Africa and the Middle East, where friars initiated some of the first interfaith conversations with Muslims. Besides celibate communities of men and women, confraternities of married people who vowed to follow the simple way of the gospel grew up in major cities.

Farther north, in what is now Belgium, groups of single women inspired by Francis joined together to form communities within the great urban centers of Leuven, Ghent, and Bruges. Known as Beguines, they established "towns within towns" that contained houses, workshops, churches, hospitals, and dorms for poorer members of the community. The women practiced celibacy, daily prayer, and simplicity, wearing plain beige dresses. Most worked in the Belgian textile factories, spending their extra time with the poor and sick. Unlike traditional nuns, the Beguines took no formal vows and shared no rule of life, but each woman promised obedience to the local community and the local pastor. Similar communities of men called the Beghards soon followed their lead. A little later, in the fourteenth century, the Brethren of the Common Life flourished in the Netherlands and Germany. Like the Beguines and the Beghards, the Brethren did not take formal vows. They roomed together in large houses and ministered to others by preaching (some were priests) and producing devotional literature. The most well-known example is *The Imitation of Christ,* by Thomas à Kempis, a book on the devotional life that has guided many people to the Way.

The (Radical) Reformation

uch movements to "monasticize" all of Christian society climaxed in the Great Reformation. The Reformers mounted a devastating critique of the "monkish" life, which was already suffering under the weight of internal problems. Luther, himself an Augustinian monk, renounced his vows, marched out of the monastery, and married a nun. Calvin likewise opposed traditional monasticism as morally and spiritually bankrupt, believing it represented a double standard for Christians – all should strive for moral perfection. Monks and nuns in reformed lands were released from their vows, and many married and joined secular life.

Meanwhile, more radical Reformers such as Michael Sattler (a former Benedictine

Marianne Stokes, *Saint Elizabeth from Hungary, Spinning for the Poor.* Elizabeth (1207–1231), a Hungarian princess, gave up her wealth to serve the poor as a member of the Third Order of Saint Francis.

Francisco de Zurbarán
Saint Francis

prior) organized new apostolic communities that rejected military service and political involvement and revived the ancient practice of believer's baptism. Among these "Anabaptists," the Mennonites considered it a mark of the true church that there should be no poor among them. The Hutterites went further, abolishing private property altogether and practicing full economic sharing. The egalitarian spirit was manifest in the practice of calling other members "brother" and "sister"; hence some groups in Moravia and Switzerland were simply called "Brethren." Persecuted across Europe by Catholics and Protestants alike, Anabaptist communities saw themselves as following in the footsteps of the persecuted early church.

The "age of exploration" opened the pathways of the sea and connected the world in previously unimaginable ways. Wherever Christians sojourned, intentional communities developed. Hundreds of Baptists and other dissenters left their homes in England and Scotland in order to build a Christian society in the New World. Both the Pilgrims who settled Plymouth Colony in 1620 and the Puritans who established the "Bible commonwealth" in the Massachusetts Bay Colony in 1630 attempted to create cohesive Christian communities. The Plymouth Pilgrims practiced the discipline of shared property in the first generation of their colony; all shared a high standard of moral discipline. The idealism of these founding communities directly influenced the formation of America's distinct sense of mission and left a legacy of utopian community, both Christian and non-Christian, in the New World.

Many of these New World communities had a millenarian cast – they believed the Second Coming was at hand. The austere community of Bohemia Manor, founded in the 1680s in Pennsylvania by the followers of Jean de Labadie (the "second Calvin"), had no private property and shared common work on the estate; food and dress were plain. A few years later, the Seventh Day Baptists established a community, also in Pennsylvania, called Ephrata Cloister. Perhaps most successful were the Shakers, established right before the Revolutionary War. By the 1830s they had attracted some four thousand members to more than sixty celibate communes called "families" in nearly twenty different settlements from Maine to Indiana. One community remains, at Sabbathday Lake, Maine. Other North American communities likewise attracted thousands: German Pietists flocked to communities such as Harmony and Economy in Pennsylvania, and New Harmony in Indiana. Another German sect, the Inspirationists, built seven communal villages in Amana,

Iowa, in the 1850s, which survived until the Great Depression. The largest intentional Christian communities in the New World are the Hutterites, who fled oppression in Europe and established expansive farming colonies on the western plains of the United States and Canada. Today there are around forty thousand Hutterites living in more than four hundred colonies.

A Living Tradition

he twentieth century witnessed a revival of radical Christian community. Communal life focused on discipleship was seen as a way to heal the wounds left by centuries of religious strife and political turmoil. In response to the church's complicity in war, Eberhard Arnold founded the Bruderhof community in Sannerz, Germany, in 1920. A few years later, in 1933, Dorothy Day and Peter Maurin founded the Catholic Worker, a community committed to serving the homeless poor. In 1934, Dietrich Bonhoeffer started the experimental underground Christian community in Finkenwald, which would become the subject of his book, *Life Together*. In 1938, a Presbyterian pastor named George MacLeod founded the Iona Community in Scotland, in order to close the gap between middle- and working-class Christians. In 1946, Roger Schütz, known as Brother Roger, founded the Taizé Community in France as an ecumenical religious order of Catholics and Protestants. A year later, Basilea Schlink, a Lutheran, founded the Evangelical Sisterhood of Mary in Darmstadt, Germany, with a mission to repent for the Holocaust and work for reconciliation between Jews and German Christians. Around the same time, the Focolare movement was emerging in Italy, and what is now the Catholic Integrated Community began in Germany. In 1964, Jean Vanier

The Taizé Community, France

founded L'Arche, an international community consisting of households of people with disabilities and their helpers. Many charismatic and activist communities also sprang up in this period, centered on Jesus' Sermon on the Mount and transcending old denominational lines. In the last several decades the New Friars, the New Monastics, and a plethora of similar urban and neo-Anabaptist missional endeavors in North America have blended elements of the active and contemplative traditions in an effort to incorporate God's kingdom into everyday life.

The communities mentioned here are but a sampling of the thousands of groups of Christians who have determined to live lives of intentional discipleship in communities modeled on the Jerusalem church. The stories of many of these communities, especially those outside of Europe and North America, remain to be told. And doubtless many communities quietly serving others will remain forever unknown. Though each community's narrative is of value in itself and worthy of remembrance, each is also a chapter in the overarching and ongoing story of Christians on the Way – a people walking many different roads with the same intention and the same destination, each group seeking to experience the presence and power of God in the shared life of community, a preparation for great communion to come. ➤

The Friars of Manhattan

JAMAL HULEATT

Father Gabriel serving lunch at the Thursday soup kitchen in St. Joseph Friary, Manhattan.

When I told the cab driver my destination, he peppered me with questions. For starters, what was a friary – something most people identify with medieval times – doing in the middle of Harlem? I found out when I arrived at St. Joseph Friary, a red brick building on West 142nd Street. "Every community must have a particular purpose," Father Gabriel, the friar responsible for St. Joseph, explained, "and this community's

vocation is to serve the poor. How could we serve those in need if we were not living among them? Our presence here gives dignity to those who need our help."

The friars and postulants living at St. Joseph Friary belong to the Franciscan Friars of the Renewal, an order founded in 1987 by eight Capuchin friars. Concerned by increasing secularism and wealth among the Capuchins, they sought to emulate Francis of Assisi, who

Jamal Huleatt, who graduated from high school in 2015, is volunteering at Fox Hill Bruderhof in Walden, New York.

Photograph by Jamal Huleatt

spent his life helping the poor. Following his example, they left behind their personal possessions and started looking for people who needed help. From their beginnings in a troubled South Bronx neighborhood, they have grown to around 130 members, with friaries on three continents.

The Franciscan Friars of the Renewal living at St. Joseph open their doors every Thursday to share a meal with the hungry. At eleven o'clock, men and women trickle in off the street and find their way down the narrow hall to the dining room. Once everyone is seated at the wooden tables, a gray-robed friar blesses the food and the soup is served. "It is Folish soup," Father Gabriel explained, handing me a bowl, "because it was made by a postulant from France, and another from Poland."

As we ate, Frank, an older man, was eager to talk. After growing up in Harlem, he'd worked on and off as a security guard, making minimum wage. Now, he said, he lives by himself, sometimes on the streets. "I come to the monks whenever I need some food. I know they're always gonna be here to help. They're the only good thing in this whole area."

Across the table from us, another man, Steve, had finished his soup and joined in: "I love coming to see the brothers because they are so hardworking and funny. They pray for people, they visit people, and they are not afraid to live here with us." When I asked Steve why he thought the friars gave up their former lives to live together in Harlem, he replied, "All these brothers are here because they want to do God's work and be his messengers. If they weren't here, who would visit us?"

The guests at the soup kitchen were unrestrained in their praise for the friars. They pointed out that volunteers at most soup kitchens travel home to richer, safer areas. By contrast, as Harlem residents, the Franciscans are very much a part of the community they serve.

Franciscan friars, who take their vow of poverty quite literally, are perhaps best known for their austerity. Their simple sandals, signature gray habits, and beards make them easy to spot in any crowd. Even the friary's cars must be modest. When I asked Father Gabriel if giving up one's phone, credit card, and car keys to become a friar is difficult, he said the vow of poverty is the easiest to keep. Friars become accustomed to a simple lifestyle, he said, and material possessions cease to have much attraction after a time.

The hardest rule, according to Father Gabriel, is obedience. As he put it, "conforming your whole will to Christ" is not easy in a culture that holds independence in such high regard, and in a city where every billboard and shop window encourages you to be yourself. By joining the community of friars, these men are making a choice to let the Holy Spirit guide their lives. Yes, letting go of the steering wheel is hard, Father Gabriel suggested, but the reward – having brothers who can help guide you – makes it worthwhile.

The friars at St. Joseph also take a vow of chastity, opting to remain celibate so that they can serve God more fully. Jesus' words in the Gospel of Matthew, chapter 19, and Paul's letters to the church in Corinth form the basis of this vow. In 1 Corinthians 7:37, Paul writes that "if a man has the willpower not to marry and decides that he doesn't need to and won't, he has made a wise decision" because "an unmarried man can spend his time doing the Lord's work and thinking how to please him." Because they don't have spouses or children, the friars have more time to pray, visit people in need, and serve the poor. According to Father

Gabriel, giving up marriage has also given him what he calls "spiritual fathership" in the lives of couples he counsels at a nearby church.

When I asked Father Gabriel why the friars live together in a community, rather than spread out among those they seek to serve, he pointed out that they are not called to live as hermits, but rather they live together to help each other. It would be difficult, he suggested, to maintain the Franciscan life of prayer, service, and poverty without support. Indeed, the friars' lives are intensely communal. From the time they enter the friary as postulants, they spend most of their day together. Religious classes, mealtimes, and recreational activities are all seen as chances to encourage and serve one another. By living and praying together, the friars enrich each other.

Of course, living in such close quarters is not always easy. I asked Brother Rufino, the friar in charge of the postulants' education, if tensions ever arise. He responded with a story from his time as a postulant, when he was put in a group with a brother he couldn't stand.

Incapable of seeing eye to eye with this other postulant but unable to avoid him in the small friary, Brother Rufino prayed that they would be put in different houses. After bringing the conflict to God, Brother Rufino was suddenly able to see this man as a brother, and they learned to love each other. Still, God humored his request, and they were placed in different houses after being confirmed.

After spending a day among the friars, one ceases to view them as indistinguishable in their beards and gray-hooded robes. Yes, they seek to become one body in Christ, and they all feel the same call to serve the poor, but they each have a unique journey that brought them to the Franciscan Friars. Father Gabriel's parents, for example, were Palestinian refugees who, after a stretch in a Jordanian refugee camp, traveled to America. They worked hard to give their children a brighter economic future than they had experienced. Imagine, then, their dismay when their son announced his intention to reject the American dream and live a life of voluntary poverty. But Father Gabriel, as part of the friary, is doing work he loves in a community of brothers who, like him, heard a call from God and answered it. As Saint Francis himself did some eight hundred years ago, today these friars provide comfort and support to those in need, in the heart of New York City and beyond. ⤳

Learn more about the Franciscan Friars of the Renewal at www.franciscanfriars.com.

American Hospitality

In rural Georgia, Jubilee Partners offers refugees and other immigrants a home and a community.

SAM HINE

With over sixty million people worldwide displaced by violence, how to treat refugees has become one of the great moral issues of our time. Yes, the Bible calls us to welcome the stranger. But what can even the best-intentioned person do in the face of unprecedented mass migration? Jubilee Partners, a community dedicated for decades to welcoming suffering people who have been displaced by war and other disasters, demonstrates that a Christian community can give support in ways an individual citizen never could.

Jubilee Partners grew out of Koinonia Farm, the Georgia community founded by Clarence Jordan and others in 1942 with a commitment to racial reconciliation and sustainable agriculture. In 1979, three years after helping to launch the house-building organization Habitat for Humanity, Koinonia's members set out to establish a new community. They chose 260 beautiful but undeveloped acres in northeast Georgia.

During their first months there, Jubilee Partners' six founding members listened to news reports about thousands of Vietnamese boat people seeking refuge in America. Living in tents themselves, with no hot showers, they resonated with the boat people's plight, and decided to respond.

On a recent visit to *Plough's* editorial offices, Don Mosley, one of those founding members, reflected on how much has changed – and how much hasn't – in the thirty-seven years since. "In the beginning, people were scared of us. The local newspaper did a headline story – an exposé, the editor called it – on this commune moving into the area. The reporter who came out and did the story went back and said, 'There's nothing there to expose. These are really nice people who want to help people!'" Today local relations couldn't be better, Mosley says.

A Melting Pot

Even before the first Vietnamese arrived, a refugee agency asked Jubilee Partners to take in migrants from Cuba. Since then, the community has hosted about four thousand refugees from more than three dozen countries, teaching English and basic skills for life in the United States, and helping with paperwork. The refugees live a short distance from the community center, offering them the space they need. Sipping coffee on his porch,

Refugees and Jubilee staff lead the local Christmas parade in Comer, Georgia.

Don Mosley loves to watch the cultural and language barriers fall away as children from Burma, the Congo, Central America, and the United States play soccer together.

To respond to the crush of migrants fleeing wars in Central America in the 1980s, Jubilee Partners bought a bus and for eight years shuttled back and forth to South Texas, where they interviewed arrivals and selected strong candidates for asylum. Though the United States, as a signatory to the United Nations' 1967 refugee protocol, agrees to grant asylum to people fleeing persecution, most Central Americans are denied refugee status on the pretext that they are migrating primarily for economic reasons. "We brought thirteen hundred Salvadorans and Guatemalans and a few Hondurans through Jubilee," Mosley recalls. "The United States rejected them, but we managed to get them legally through the United States, and the Canadians accepted them."

About a quarter of the refugees who have passed through Jubilee Partners are Muslim. They are invited to attend the community's Christian prayer services, but are also offered transportation to the nearest mosque. Many Muslim refugees, such as those from Bosnia, fled persecution from Christians. "We don't

hear that side of it very much in this country," Mosley says. "In one case, a man came to us with scars all over his chest, crosses. He said a man stood there and carved those crosses on his chest with a knife and said, 'I'm converting you to a Christian.'" At Jubilee Partners, these victims see a different face of Christianity, and healing begins. One Muslim man told Mosley and his wife, Carolyn, "I feel that I have actually seen Jesus here."

After a Cuban refugee died of a heart attack at Jubilee Partners, the community started a cemetery. Later, community members began to visit people on Georgia's death row, something they continue to do frequently. They offer these prisoners burial in that same little cemetery, should they end up being executed. So far, at least six such individuals have been buried there. Don Mosley says, "I'll be very honored if someday my remains are out there among all those death row folks and Congolese and Burmese and whomever."

Beyond Borders

As they listened to refugees' stories, Jubilee Partners decided that helping new arrivals was not enough; they had to do something about the root causes. In the years since, Don Mosley has led dozens of delegations of journalists and church leaders into war zones to better understand what causes people to flee their homes. This has often led to relief efforts, education programs, and other attempts to address these problems.

Working to change perceptions back home in the United States has proved even more challenging. Mosley says, "I think we're much too concerned about protecting our money or our advantages. Boundaries are necessary to some degree here and there, but if the emphasis were more on how can we address what's causing those beautiful kids to be driven away from home and many of them killed in the process as they try to come up through Mexico for instance, or to Greece from Turkey, we could do a lot to diminish the problem and the numbers of people. They would rather stay home if they could. They're not fleeing because they want to be American. That's a distortion. They're fleeing because they're being driven out by violence and danger."

Meanwhile, Back in Georgia

The richest part of being at Jubilee Partners, Mosley says, is getting to know not only the refugees but the many people, young and old, who come to volunteer from around the United States and around the world – "getting to know these people well, hearing their spiritual backgrounds, their family struggles, falling in love with more and more people."

Still, Mosley is quick to admit to challenges. The community struggles to maintain continuity with a high turnover of refugees and volunteers, and the work can be taxing. "It's a small community, and at times we're practically outnumbered by just the refugees themselves. In addition to that, we have anywhere from a thousand to two thousand visitors a year. There are about twenty adults,

referred to as 'resident partners,' who live at Jubilee year-round. We could easily work too hard. We have to pace ourselves."

In addition, Mosley's peacemaking and fundraising efforts mean he is often traveling. How does a man in his late seventies manage these various roles? "When I'm home, I try to walk three or four miles a day," he says. "I attend the prayer time almost every morning and make room for worship time and quiet time. I try to mix those kinds of healing, celebrating, appreciating-God's-world-around-us activities with the more routine and even difficult things that have to be done. I take my turn on dishes and cooking and all the rest just like everyone else. And somehow it all flows together. We've got enough people who are ready to play a good game of soccer or, if it's cold outside, Scrabble or something. There's laughter, there's music, there are guitars, a cello, and a piano. It's a rich life. I wouldn't trade it for five hundred thousand dollars a year. Forget it. I had that option as a young guy, and I'm glad I chose this instead."

Asked if he had a message for the young people who will hopefully carry on the work he has started, Mosley says, "By all means, try out a life of community in one form or another, a life of serving, whether it's in the Peace Corps or any other type of volunteer agency, international or local. Go out and find out how rich that kind of life is. Don't let yourself get channeled into 'I'm going to make a lot of money as soon as I can get the right credentials, and buy a house out in an isolated suburb.' That's a miserable way to live compared to living together, one way or another." ⤳

To learn more about Jubilee Partners and Don Mosley's international peacemaking work, read his book Faith beyond Borders: Doing Justice in a Dangerous World *(Abingdon, 2010). Watch our interview with him at* plough.com/mosley.

The Luxury of Being Surprised

Notes from a Failed Missionary on Rediscovering Faith

D. L. MAYFIELD

A few years ago, my small family planted ourselves in the most diverse neighborhood in all of America, soaking up the differences while striving for commonalities. Our new neighborhood had a rich history of African American and Native American populations, and it was also a space where wave after wave of immigrants and refugees crashed on the shores a decade or two after the wars in their own countries caused them to seek asylum.

In our new apartment, our new neighborhood, we were thrilled as only white people can be, gentrifiers in every sense of the word, experiencing the benefits of diverse cultures and cheap rent while having no knowledge or experience in the systemic injustices that governed the lives of many of our new neighbors. While we had lived in low-income housing before, we still managed to view it all as a bit of a lark, an "experiment" in downward mobility.

Photograph by Sean M. O'Grady, *New Orleans Shotgun Double*

But things change when you allow the experience of your neighbors to shape you, instead of the other way around. We started to see how things that were fraught with complications for many of our neighbors were easy for us: obtaining fair housing, experiencing limited interactions with the police (who were always respectful to us), having access to fair-wage jobs, and enjoying a much lower propensity to be caught (and charged) for minor civil infractions. For a while, we were unable to comprehend what we were seeing and experiencing as bystanders in a divided America. Eventually, the weight of the truth started to settle on our shoulders, calling a grief that we never knew was in us, a form of lament that threated to overwhelm us if we let it.

And one day, it did.

The day our neighbor came over and watched my husband and me pour our spirits out was a day that forever changed me. Grieved and imprisoned by our own wounds, the persistent lies we were fed and had nurtured, the histories that we swallowed whole, the sins as old as time, we pleaded with him to help us understand. There was a black boy who died, and the person who killed him was let go. Our neighbor stayed for coffee and let us talk, and then he said: *"You have the luxury of being surprised. Nobody else around here is."* In his astounding kindness my neighbor stayed and talked with us, patient and sorrowful, his weariness more harrowing to my soul than I could begin to understand. That one sentence – *You have the luxury of being surprised* – will stay with me the rest of my life, a testament to privilege I no longer want.

My choice of neighborhoods is just the start of me trying to scale the large mountains of alienation that are inside of me. I feel like I see the wounds of Christ bright red in front of me, but I am still not able to feel them.

That people prefer themselves and all others like them is not a surprise to any of us, but I am consistently taken aback at how often we refuse to acknowledge that our systems (political and religious) might have the same kind of problem. Being the minority where I work and live and play has opened my eyes to the way the systems are intrinsically *for me.* This never bothered me until I realized what the converse of that equation is: those systems are actively against others.

That realization alone is enough to stop me. The words *sin* and *repentance* and *judgment* are infused with new meaning. True repentance, I was always taught, involves turning away from myself and turning toward God. Now, it has meant turning toward the ones who are being shut out.

It is this: moving in, listening, reading books. Putting myself in a position to be wrong, to be silent, to be chastised, to be extended forgiveness, to withhold judgment, to invite understanding. I thought the cost would be steep, but it has turned out to be the opposite. *You have the luxury of being surprised.* And surprised I have been – how I have seen and heard and felt the Spirit convict me, how I am starting to understand how unwell I have been all this time. And the flip side is this: as it turns out, I am exactly the kind of person Jesus came for. He can only heal us once we figure out that we can't be of any use at all. ⇘

D. L. Mayfield and her husband work with refugee communities in Portland, Oregon. This article is taken from Mayfield's new book Assimilate or Go Home: Notes from a Failed Missionary on Rediscovering Faith *(HarperOne, August 2016).*

The Incident in Changu's Pepper Patch

Kwon Jeong-saeng

Illustrated by Kim Dong-sung ◇ Translated by Raymond Mommsen

IT'S MIDSUMMER and the cicadas buzzing languidly in the shade of the oak trees sound like an old man sawing wood. Just over the hill behind the oak trees is Changu's pepper patch.

Since early spring, Changu's mother and older sister have been panting up and down that hill, carrying chamber pots and baskets of manure to fertilize the field. They have sweated

Kwon Jeong-saeng (1937–2007) spent his childhood as a Korean War refugee and later became a beloved children's author. A passionate advocate for children victimized by war, he continued to live in a simple one-room dwelling near his village church, which he served as bell ringer (see his autobiographical essay "The Church I Dreamed Of" in our Autumn 2014 issue). At his death, he left all his lifetime savings to children in need, especially those in North Korea.

in streams while pulling weeds. The pepper plants have grown huge. The plants don't seem to mind all the gravel in the soil. They hold up their leaves, spread their branches, and open their white flowers. Finally cute baby peppers come to hang in bunches. The little peppers drink the spicy wind from the mountain and try to make their faces beautiful.

"You look like an elephant's nose."

"What elephant has a nose this small?"

"I mean a toy elephant."

"So what do you think you look like then?"

Baby peppers really do look like the trunk of a tiny elephant. They change from pale green to dark green. And then they change into their red suits.

No, that's not right. The color is from inside. It's not like clothes they put on: the glow from their pure, fiery hearts blazes through until you can see it from the outside.

At midday, when the cicadas are droning under the oak trees, the red noses all flare up together like tongues of flame. If you go near the pepper patch, your nose burns and your eyes sting – and don't even think about touching them.

On a day just like this, Changu's mother is sitting by the pepper patch with her next-door neighbor.

"These days, if you look away for a second, somebody will steal the eyes out of your head."

"What are you talking about?"

"Haven't you heard about the pepper thief? They say he comes in the middle of the night, fills a sack with peppers, and runs off."

"How terrible! He must be crazy."

"Not just everyday-crazy either. Completely insane. It's frightening."

"Who's lost their peppers then?"

"In the village across the river, a bunch of different fields have been robbed."

"You better be careful too."

"I can't watch for thieves every night."

The two women go down the hill together, and the red toy-elephant's noses snort out a spicy blast of rage at the very thought.

"This is intolerable!"

"Intolerable, but it can happen."

"Can happen, but it's intolerable."

"Heaven will punish the scoundrel."

"Heaven better punish him!"

The peppers have all been talking at once, and now they snap their mouths shut. They realize that it could happen to them too, and fear almost freezes their hearts. That very night the thief might come and take them captive.

"I wish we had hands and feet."

"So you could run away?"

"Don't be stupid. I'd fight."

"Fight the thief?"

"Sure."

"But we're stuck on the pepper plants. We can't even move."

"We can get mad can't we?"

"Getting mad is childish. Let's be courageous."

"Courageous?"

"Right. Little peppers are spicy, aren't they? We can use that if we're smart."

The more the peppers talk, the more agitated they get, as if the thief might burst into the patch at any moment. That night, they don't sleep at all. As they stare wide-eyed into the night, their faces get redder and redder. For four nights they watch, ready for battle at any moment. Toward evening one day, Changu's mother comes up the hill.

"Well, the peppers are finally ripe. Tomorrow I'll bring Changu, and we'll pick them together." She quickly looks over the patch and goes home, and the peppers relax a bit.

"I guess we don't need to worry now."

"Looks like the hand that planted will get the harvest after all."

They swing happily back and forth, shaking the branches of their plants. The oil on their skin gleams in the light of the setting sun. They are so happy that they are full grown and will be harvested by their rightful owner that their hearts are nearly bursting.

That night the stars are unusually thick and bright, scattered across heaven like shards of glass. The pepper babies are sleeping peacefully, exhausted after four nights of watching.

The night grows silently darker.

It is darkest under the oak trees.

A black shadow crawls up the slope under the cover of the black forest. A strange shadow – it has a horrible burlap sack in its hand. It creeps to the edge of the pepper patch and slowly stands up and looks all around. But nothing moves in the darkness.

The shadow sinks down between the rows of plants and its hands work quickly. The sleeping peppers feel themselves being grabbed and come awake with a shock. The shadow grabs everything, even half-ripened green peppers, and stuffs them roughly into his sack, stripping the branches clean. The terrible sack begins to stretch.

"Save the peppers!"

"The thief is taking us!"

The peppers scream, but it is no use. How could the thief be so pitiless, so utterly lacking any human feeling? He snatches everything his hands touches, even ripping off branches, and stuffs his sack to the brim. In no time, Changu's pepper patch is empty. The thief ties the mouth of the sack tightly and throws it over his shoulder, stuffed so tight it seems ready to burst.

In the sack, the peppers are helpless as the thief hurries down the mountain path. They think about how for days they have bragged about fighting the thief, only to be dragged off without a struggle. There has to be a way to escape.

They are jammed in the sack so tightly they can't even wiggle, but one pepper calls out:

"Hey, what are we going to do?"

The other peppers start shouting.

"We can't just go quietly!"

"Think of Changu's poor mother."

"She worked so hard so we could grow big."

"We belong to Changu's family."

The peppers' fiery blood begins to boil in righteous fury.

"Fight, fight against this injustice!"

They wriggle and pant in desperation. The sack begins to swell. The thief can hardly walk. The sack stretches further, puffing up like a balloon. The thief grunts and gasps.

The peppers yell together at the top of their voices, "Heave-ho! Heave-ho!"

The thief struggles down the dark path, sweat gushing down his face.

The sack is swollen to its limit, ready to burst at the slightest touch.

As he passes under the oak tree where the night is darkest, the thief has to feel his way one step at a time. A field mouse runs through the grass by his feet and he jumps back in fright. His foot slips on a rock covered with wet moss, and he falls to the ground. The sack swings against the rock and explodes with a deafening sound. Peppers fly everywhere.

"Hurray, we're free!"

Just then, the wind blows up the mountainside, and the flying peppers catch the wind and sail back up the hill like a flock of ravens. They flash in the starlight, lighting up the night sky like fireworks.

Then they fall quivering to earth, and each one goes quietly back to the branch it came from. A few change places and land on someone else's branch, and some even hang upside down. But they don't mind, and the peppers smile contentedly.

The night mist falls silently and the eastern sky turns grey. As morning comes, the peppers seem to hang even more beautifully than before.

Later in the day Changu's mother and big sister come and lovingly pick the ripe, red peppers.

Editors' Picks

Laurus
Eugene Vodolazkin
(Oneworld Publications)

Readers who are short on time are often quick to ignore new novels in favor of recent nonfiction (small-talk-enabling) and classics (reliable). *Laurus,* the novel by Russian medievalist Eugene Vodolazkin, is a powerful reason to resist this temptation. It tells the story of a boy born in 1440 who is baptized as Arseny, loses his parents to the plague, and as an adolescent inherits his grandfather's practice as herbalist and medicine man. As Arseny passes through life, changing names as he goes, he is variously a father, a penitent, a faith healer, a prophet, a holy fool, a pilgrim, and finally, a saint.

Colorful and earthy, this is no pious tale, yet it is suffused with a sense of the interwovenness of the invisible and the material worlds. Prayer, it becomes clear, is far more potent than Arseny's medical arts; by the end of the book, he discards his herbs completely. Just as real is the continuing presence of those who have died among the living. It is Arseny's desire to do penance on behalf of Ustina, the unmarried mother of his son who died in childbirth without the sacrament of confession, that impels him to a life of holiness and self-sacrifice.

Lisa C. Hayden's translation from Russian, which reflects the original's mix of colloquialisms and archaic language, is generally fluent and compelling. (One quibble: the pastiches of Chaucerian English can be irritatingly amateurish.) All in all, *Laurus* is one of those rare books that can help us live our lives with a greater degree of "assurance of things hoped for, and the certainty of things unseen."

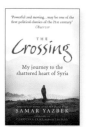

The Crossing: My Journey to the Shattered Heart of Syria
Samar Yazbek
(Ebury Press)

In Yazbek's Syria, terrifying nightmares, imagined and concrete, run into one another seamlessly. In Homs, the streets are impassable, filled with smoking rubble, toxic dust, and the stench of burned flesh. In the countryside near Aleppo, the beauty of a spring orchard hides snipers lurking among the blossoms.

A Syrian journalist, Yazbek gives scant space to the politics behind the conflict. Her goal is different: to record the shattering stories of her people, from grandmothers and teens to militants (she interviewed more than fifty) – no matter their allegiance. It's a risky business. In one chilling scene, she interviews a prominent emir of the Islamic State. Sweating with fear, but unable to just sit there and listen to him, she tells him that his views are "absolutely evil." Unbelievably, he simply dismisses her, saying, "Leave the war to us men, sister."

At times Yazbek wonders how effective her efforts are. How long, she agonizes, will the blood go on pooling in Syria's streets and cellars while the world looks on, transfixed, but unable or unwilling to stop the war? No one can answer that. But when the tide turns, it will be thanks in part to the power of stories such as these.

For stories specifically about Christians persecuted by ISIS, there's *They Say We Are Infidels* (Tyndale Momentum), in which journalist and *World* magazine editor Mindy Belz gives on-the-ground reporting and perspectives on what it means to be Christian in the Middle East today.

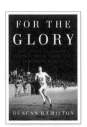

For the Glory: Eric Liddell's Journey from Olympic Champion to Modern Martyr
Duncan Hamilton
(Penguin Press)

The defining chapter of Eric Liddell's life is not the one immortalized by the classic film *Chariots of Fire*. In the film, the twenty-two-year-old Scottish champion refuses to run the 100 meters in the 1924 Paris Olympics because the race is scheduled on a Sunday, then goes on to win gold at 400 meters, beating his nearest competitor by a whopping seven yards.

The film misses the more amazing story of the life that followed Liddell's decision to renounce celebrity and a gold-studded athletic career to become a missionary in a remote Chinese village. The grinding poverty in Siaochang, where Liddell had spent his own early childhood as the son of missionaries, took a turn for the worse with the arrival of civil war and Japanese occupation; the danger would separate Liddell from his wife and daughters for the better part of their marriage.

During World War II the Japanese imprisoned Liddell and 1,800 other foreign nationals in Weihsien, a camp that measured a mere 150 by 200 yards. (Another prisoner, Langdon Gilkey, recounts the exceptional communal life that emerged from this duress in his 1966 book *Shantung Compound*.) Here Liddell gave his last ounce to keep fellow prisoners' hope alive, dying at age forty-three of an inoperable brain tumor.

In Duncan Hamilton's impressive new biography, Liddell seems larger than life at times, the biographer awed by the seemingly superhuman goodness of his subject. But through eyes of faith, the irrepressible positivity, dedication, and compassion Liddell demonstrates even in dire situations gives glory to God, who gives such strength of character to mere mortals who are willing to die to self and allow him to work through them.

Evicted: Poverty and Profit in the American City
Matthew Desmond
(Crown Publishers)

He may be a Harvard sociologist, but he's also an exceptional journalist. In what could prove to be among the most important books of 2016, Desmond shows how housing evictions disrupt the lives of the poorest Americans, who are paying up to 80 percent of their income to rent substandard accommodation in the nation's worst neighborhoods. He compares the impact of eviction in the lives of black women and children to that of incarceration in the lives of young black men: "Poor black men are locked up; poor black women are locked out."

Before writing, Desmond spent a year living in a trailer park and an urban ghetto in Milwaukee, following tenants to court, homeless shelters, and funerals, and listening to landlords explain how they find it impossible to build new housing at affordable prices.

"Decent affordable housing should be a basic right." Desmond writes. "Without stable shelter, everything else falls apart." But his stories show how other factors, such as family breakdown, mass incarceration, drug addiction, and unemployment all conspire to send people into a downward spiral that leaves them and their possessions back on the sidewalk.

Desmond makes some specific proposals, such as vouchers to make up for the shortfall in public housing – currently four times as many people qualify as can be accommodated and the wait is counted in years and even decades. At the same time, *Evicted* shows just how hard it will be to solve this silent crisis. But that doesn't mean we shouldn't try. The tragic human stories told here demand a response. ➤ *The Editors*

The Jesus Indians of Ohio

CRAIG D. ATWOOD

As the American War of Independence raged, Christian settlers and Native Americans lived together as brothers and sisters – and paid the ultimate price for their nonviolent discipleship.

Christian Schussele, *Zeisberger Preaching to the Indians,* 1862

On November 24, 1755, ten Moravian missionaries and a child were murdered at Gnadenhütten, Pennsylvania, near modern-day Lehighton, on Mahoning Creek. Susanne Luise Partsch, who had recently come to Gnadenhütten with her husband George, saw men "running from one house to another with firebrands to set them alight."[1] A Native American war party burned the church, school, bakery, and dwellings to the ground, and burned several residents, including an infant, alive in their homes. The cattle were slaughtered, while stores, tools, and supplies were taken or ruined. One woman whose husband was killed in the raid was seized; while in captivity, she was raped and abused so severely that she never fully recovered. Susanne Partsch survived by leaping from a second-story window, fleeing, and taking shelter under a hollow tree. A local militia member found her the next morning and returned her to the settlement. She wrote of her experience, "I fainted at the sight of the charred bodies, and they had trouble bringing me back to my senses."[2]

The massacre of the mainly German missionaries was a minor event in a much larger conflict between France and England called the Seven Years' War. The North American theater of this conflict was known as the French and Indian War, during which American colonists fought alongside British troops and their Native American allies against the French and their Native American allies. Native American tribes were forced to decide between fighting for the British or resisting them. For some Native Americans, most notably the Delaware chief Teedyuscung, the war presented an opportunity to reclaim ancestral lands the British had stolen. Teedyuscung had converted to Christianity before the war and lived with the Moravians at Gnaddenhütten for some time, but when the Delaware were attacked by other tribes, the Moravians urged them not to resist, which offended Teedyuscung. He rejected Moravian pacifism and began raiding white and Native American settlements.

Only twelve days before the massacre, on November 12, the Moravians had decided, despite signs of impending violence, that it was "better that a Brother should die at his post than withdraw and have a single soul thus suffer loss."[3] The Moravian missionary John Martin Mack, who had devoted his life to ministering to native peoples, had encouraged the missionaries at Gnadenhütten ("houses of grace") to remain at their post. (On hearing the news of the slaughter, he was heartbroken, yet still joined other Moravians in urging their friends among the Delaware not to seek revenge on their behalf.)

The day after the assault, the Moravian congregation in Bethlehem, Pennsylvania, was summoned at dawn for daily prayer with the ringing of the church bell. Bishop August Gottlieb Spangenberg read the Bible verse designated for the day from Genesis 42: "Joseph made himself strange unto them and spake roughly unto them." The bishop told the congregation that sometimes God speaks roughly and seems strange, "but we know his heart." With a quavering voice, he informed the congregation of the martyrdom of their brothers and sisters at Gnadenhütten, twenty-five miles to the northwest. The congregation prayed and wept. Soon Native American and white refugees from the Blue Mountains, including George and Susanne Partsch, began arriving in Bethlehem, seeking food, shelter, and protection. Susanne felt "wretched and had to bear a serious illness."

In all, about eight hundred people made their way to Bethlehem and nearby Nazareth, a rare instance of Europeans and Native Americans in the eighteenth century seeking shelter together. Moravian historian Joseph Mortimer Levering notes that the presence of seventy Native American refugees from Gnadenhütten "put a strain upon the confidence and good will of some of the Bethlehem people, under the poignant grief they felt for the awful fate that had befallen their brethren and sisters on the Mahoning; all on account of Indians and at the hands of Indians; and under the growing dread of an attack upon Bethlehem."[4] Despite

---

Craig D. Atwood is associate professor and director of the Center for Moravian Studies at the Moravian Theological Seminary in Bethlehem, Pennsylvania. This account is one of thirty-six in Plough's new book Bearing Witness: Stories of Martyrdom and Costly Discipleship.

their anxiety, Bishop Spangenberg urged the Brethren not to close their hearts to the refugees, who had been driven from their homes by violence, and so the Moravians, sometimes

In this nineteenth-century illustration, Native American Moravians in Ohio pray as a white militia begins to execute them.

reluctantly, continued to protect the Native Americans from whites intent on revenge.

To relieve overcrowding in the Bethlehem commune, the Moravians helped the Native Americans build a village called Nain a mile from town, where they could live according to their traditional economy while still worshiping as Moravians. It took a while to find a suitable spot and clear the land for building, but finally, in October 1758, the village chapel was dedicated. Some non-Moravian whites took issue with Nain, and Teedyuscung, who objected to the idea of Delawares embracing the church's pacifism, tried in vain to persuade Native Americans to leave. In 1763, the Pennsylvania Assembly insisted that the Moravians bring their Native American Brethren to Philadelphia in an attempt to protect them from the so-called Paxton Boys, a group of vigilantes responsible for murdering Native Americans. Conditions in the Philadelphia refugee camp

were grim, and eventually the Moravian missionary David Zeisberger was allowed to take a group out of Pennsylvania to settle in Ohio.

To understand the Moravian commitment to pacifism during the French and Indian War, it is important to understand the church's history. Founded in the mid-fifteenth century as the first peace church, the Moravian Church – called the Unitas Fratrum ("Unity of the Brethren") – at one time had some four hundred congregations in Bohemia, Moravia, and Poland. The church was virtually destroyed by religious persecution in the Holy Roman Empire during and after the Thirty Years' War, but a remnant survived. The last bishop of the Moravian branch of the Unitas Fratrum was Jan Amos Comenius, who, while most famous for his writings on pedagogy and child rearing, also was one of the foremost pacifist authors of the early modern period. In 1722, a group of Protestants fled persecution in Moravia and were granted refuge on the estate of Count Nikolaus von Zinzendorf.

The Moravians built a village called Herrnhut on Zinzendorf's land, and with his assistance it became a unique Christian community. Everyone who agreed to live according to the Brotherly Agreement, ratified in 1727, was welcomed regardless of church affiliation or nationality. The Brotherly Agreement stipulated that the only reason to live in Herrnhut was service to Christ. The Herrnhuters called one another "brother" and "sister," and they adopted rituals and offices modeled on the example of the earliest Christians. The rituals included foot washing, the kiss of peace, and the *agape* meal. Though they called themselves the Brüdergemeine ("Community of the Brethren"), women as well as men were chosen as the leaders of the community.

On August 13, 1727, the Herrnhuters experienced a significant spiritual transformation that inspired them to embark on an extraordinary fifty-year global mission. The first missionary, Leonard Dober, traveled to the island of St. Thomas in the West Indies in 1732. He hoped to befriend those suffering the cruelty and indignity of slavery. In 1735, the first Moravian missionaries arrived in North America and befriended Native Americans near Savannah, Georgia. (It was while he was on route to Georgia that John Wesley, the cofounder of Methodism, first encountered the Moravians.)[5] In 1740, Moravians arrived in Pennsylvania, and the next year they began the community of Bethlehem, which was to be a base of operations for an extensive network of missionaries. Dozens of Moravians learned Native American languages, and some were adopted into various tribes in the Iroquois Confederacy. Moravian men and women lived with Native Americans in villages like Shamokin, Shekomeko, and Friedenshütten.

Bethlehem was not only the economic and administrative headquarters for the Moravian mission in North America – it was intended to be a "city on the hill." The Brethren in Bethlehem built some of the largest buildings in colonial Pennsylvania to house the hundreds of men, women, and children who lived there under the Brotherly Agreement. Some residents agreed to stay permanently to raise crops and provide support for the church, while others were "pilgrims" who agreed to go where they were sent. Many of these pilgrims worked with Native Americans, especially among the Lenape, or Delaware, people. Though the influx of war refugees in the late 1750s severely strained Bethlehem's economy and social structures, the church survived. Brethren were not permitted to join the militia or serve in the army, but the church's rules did allow for self-defense and the defense of women and children. They explained to outsiders that they were neither *kriegerisch* (willing to serve in the military) nor *quäkerisch* (absolutely nonviolent); instead, they were willing to take up arms only if necessary to preserve the lives of the innocent and defenseless.[6]

On several occasions in the 1750s and 1760s, the Brethren in Bethlehem were threatened by Native American war parties and white mobs. Many colonists accused the Moravians of plotting with Native Americans and even arming them, but in fact Moravians consistently sought to be people of peace. In order to protect the town from the type of assault suffered at Gnaddenhütten, the Moravians built a stockade around Bethlehem and the neighboring community of Nazareth. Brethren kept watch day and night, with orders to fire warning shots if anyone was seen moving against the town. In a move that shocked some non-Moravian white settlers, armed Native American Brethren stood watch with white Brethren. In this way at least one raid was prevented. On Christmas Day in 1755, Bethlehem's Moravians celebrated the birth of Christ as they usually did, by playing trombones just before dawn. According to later reports, the sound of brass

Mass grave at the site of the 1782 massacre, Gnadenhütten, Ohio

instruments, often associated with armies, so alarmed a group planning a dawn assault that they aborted their mission and retreated into the woods.

In 1775, war again engulfed the British colonies in America. The Single Brothers' House in Bethlehem became a hospital for wounded soldiers from both sides, and Moravians strove to bury the war dead with dignity. Though the British Parliament had granted Moravians an exemption from military service in 1749 in recognition of their long-established pacifism, during the American Revolution Moravians often had to pay large indemnities to avoid conscription. On several occasions, both sides threatened the Moravians with forced conscription. Some Brethren were jailed; others fled.

At the site in Ohio where David Zeisberger and his wife Suzanna had brought their congregation of Lenape and Mohican Brethren from Pennsylvania, a Mohican named Joshua was now the head of the new community, named Gnadenhütten in honor of the martyrs of 1755. By the start of the Revolutionary War, the village had grown to over two hundred people, all Native American. As the conflict moved westward, the British forcibly relocated the Moravians to Sandusky in 1781. Many starved, died of disease, or froze to death during the winter. In the spring, over a hundred Brethren were allowed to return to

their villages on the Tuscarawas River where they hoped to plant crops and hunt game.

But the specter of war and hatred stalked the land. After several non-Moravian white families were massacred by Native American war parties allied with the British, an American militia of about 160 people led by David Williamson set out for revenge. Rather than seeking out the guilty, they decided to attack the innocent pacifists at Gnadenhütten. In early March 1782, they occupied Gnadenhütten and rounded up other Native Americans from surrounding villages and woods. On March 7 they held a mock tribunal, convicted the Moravian Brethren of murder, and sentenced them to death. The only mercy they showed was to honor the request of the Moravians to prepare themselves for martyrdom. Throughout the night the Native American Brethren confessed their sins, comforted one another, and sang hymns to Christ their Savior. The next day, the white militia murdered ninety-six people. Two boys who managed to hide under bodies bore witness to the atrocity and the courage of the martyrs. According to their report, there were two "killing houses," one for men and one for women. Most were killed by mallets and tomahawks, and militia members scalped many of those killed, some while they were still alive. Nearly half of the victims were children. According to one participant: "Nathan Rollins had tomahawked nineteen of the poor Moravians, & after it was over he sat down & cried, & said it was no satisfaction for the loss of his father & uncle after all."[7]

After the killing spree was over, the militia looted the town and burned the buildings with the bodies in them. Later, Moravian missionary John Heckewelder visited the site and buried the remains of the martyrs. None of the militia members who participated in the massacre were ever brought to justice, though some were killed by non-Moravian Lenape out of revenge. British authorities granted Zeisberger permission to take the remaining members of his Lenape and Mohican congregation to Canada where they would be safer. Ontario's Moraviantown traces its origins to these refugees from Ohio.

Sadly, the 1782 Gnadenhütten massacre virtually ended the fifty-year Moravian effort to bring Europeans and Native Americans together in Christian community as brothers and sisters. As news of the events there spread from tribe to tribe, Native Americans became less and less trustful of white people. Two decades later, the Shawnee chief Tecumseh reminded the future US president William Henry Harrison: "You recall the time when the Jesus Indians of the Delawares lived near the Americans, and had confidence in their promises of friendship, and thought they were secure, yet the Americans murdered all the men, women, and children, even as they prayed to Jesus?"[8]

Today, little remains of the courageous Moravian outreach to the First Peoples of North America, but several monuments to their efforts still stand. The most important of these historical markers are found near the Wyoming Valley in Pennsylvania and near the Tuscarawas River in Ohio. Both were erected by Moravians to honor those who lost their lives in the two settlements that shared a name – Gnaddenhütten. In Pennsylvania, white Moravians were killed by Native Americans. In Ohio, Native American Brethren were killed by white Americans. They were men, women, and children who tried to follow the way of Christ in a violent and dangerous time. They were men, women, and children who sang praises to their Savior, who gave his life for them. They were men, women, and children who looked past differences in skin color, language, and customs in order to call each other brother and sister. They were men, women, and children who were prepared to sacrifice their own lives rather than take the lives of others. We can view those who died in these two communities as victims or victors. For their brothers and sisters in the faith, those Moravians joined the ranks of thousands of Christian martyrs who bore witness in life and death to their faith in Christ by loving their enemies and praying for those who persecuted them. ⤚

1. Memoir of Susanne Luise Partsch, in Katherine Faull, ed. *Moravian Women's Memoirs: Their Related Lives, 1750–1820* (Syracuse University Press, 1997), 111–113.

2. Ibid.

3. Quoted in J. T. Hamilton and Kenneth G. Hamilton, *History of the Moravian Church* (Bethlehem, 1967), 142.

4. Joseph Mortimer Levering, *A History of Bethlehem, Pennsylvania 1741–1892* (Bethlehem: Times Publishing Company, 1903), 315.

5. Geordan Hammond, *John Wesley in America: Restoring Primitive Christianity* (Oxford: Oxford University Press, 2014); Colin Podmore, *The Moravian Church in England, 1728–1760* (Oxford: Clarendon Press, 1998).

6. Jared Burkholder, "Neither 'Kriegerisch' nor 'Quäkerisch': Moravians and the Question of Violence in Eighteenth-Century Pennsylvania," *Journal of Moravian History* 12 (2012): 143–169.

7. J. T. Holmes, *The American Family of Rev. Obadiah Holmes* (Columbus, Ohio: 1915).

8. Quoted in *Major Problems in American History*, vol. 1, ed. Elizabeth Cobb et al. (Cengage, 2011), 205.

PEDRO H. ARRIAGA ALARCÓN

Three Open Wounds

*The Unfinished Story of Mexico's
Pacifist Mayan Martyrs*

Nineteen years ago *this December, the world's attention was briefly drawn to the mountainous highlands of Chiapas, Mexico's poorest and southernmost state. Centuries of injustice had led to a brief armed uprising by the indigenous population in 1994. The ski-masked and bandoleered Zapatistas grabbed headlines and eventually negotiated a peace treaty, but paramilitary death squads continued to operate with impunity, sowing terror in villages suspected of being Zapatista support bases.*

Then, three days before Christmas 1997, paramilitary fighters slaughtered forty-five internally displaced Tzotzil Mayan peasants, mostly women and children, as they prayed for peace in a chapel in the village of Acteal. The victims were members of Las Abejas ("The Bees"), a Christian group committed to nonviolence. At the time, Plough *expressed hope that the massacre would mark a turning point, quoting the words of a local priest, Oscar Salinas, at a memorial service held in Acteal:*

> *These brothers and sisters of ours decided to suffocate with their own blood the growing vortex of violence that is unleashed in our state. To offer one's life as they offered theirs is the most decent act anyone has been able to do in this time and place, in which the unending chain of offenses and misunderstandings have the word of truth caught in a blind alley. The innocent martyrs of Acteal are saving us from our confusion and cowardice. Praying they died. Fasting they died. This was the death they chose, praying and fasting for all of us. We can see it. With them has been planted the seed of peace.*

Our coverage also included a heartrending personal reflection by Las Abejas' own priest, Pedro Arriaga:

> *Cursed are the poor, those who hunger, those who weep? Cursed are those who are hated, driven out, and deemed criminals for the sake of the Son of Man? Where, in all this darkness, is God's promised justice? . . . The reaction within my bowels turns demoniac: I reject the cross of suffering and death. What am I here for? Have I come to die also? I resist having my life taken unjustly. I cannot understand the murder of the peaceful, those who refuse to take up weapons. . . .*

We recently asked Father Arriaga how his community has fared in the two decades since. He wrote in response:

A few weeks after the massacre of forty-five Tzotzil indigenous in Chiapas, a memorial entitled *An Open Wound* was published. It included photos of each of the victims: babies in their mother's arms, adolescents, adults, and elderly. There are twenty women, four of them pregnant; sixteen children; and nine men.

Those of us who were close to them, living with the survivors in the following days, wept and prayed, left helpless by this genocide.

We had been living in this violent atmosphere long before December 22, 1997, when the paramilitary forces attacked a prayer meeting beginning a three-day fast for peace in a Catholic church in Acteal. For three months there had been organized violence: house burnings and sporadic assassinations had forced ten thousand to flee their communities. Fifteen days before, a dialogue had been opened in an effort to stop the escalating violence, but to no avail.

Opposite: Members of Las Abejas issue a demand to the Mexican army to stop occupying their communities (2013).

Pedro H. Arriaga Alarcón, SJ, serves as a parish priest and episcopal vicar in the Diocese of San Cristobal de las Casas in Chiapas, Mexico.

Photograph courtesy of NetoRules

A child from Acteal marches in support of the forty-three Mexican students kidnapped from Ayotzinapa, Mexico (2014).

So as not to sully its own image, the Mexican army had created eleven paramilitary groups in different areas of Chiapas. The one in Los Altos de Chiapas was called The Red Mask. Its strategy was to enlist unemployed men by offering them a clandestine training. It succeeded in recruiting both Protestants and Catholics.

The Red Mask had already chosen to target Las Abejas, a pacifist civil society that had formed in 1992 in response to the ideal of social commitment preached by Samuel Ruíz García, bishop of the Diocese of San Cristóbal de las Casas, and guided by the light of the Word of God. While rejecting the violence of the Zapatista Army of National Liberation (EZLN), Las Abejas did stand in solidarity with EZLN's demands for justice in the uprising on January 1, 1994. Likewise, they participated in the peace talks with the federal government at San Andres. Although the Mexican government signed agreements at the peace talks, they never actually acted on their promises. All this has left the community with three open wounds.

The first wound against the pacifist indigenous – the 1997 massacre – remains open because the perpetrators still live in impunity. There has been no reconciliation between the victims and the perpetrators. Around eighty of the accused have been released because of a revision in the legal process, leaving no determination as to their guilt. Their release was like rubbing salt into the wound.

The second wound, division, has lacerated the heart of the community. It is a living wound that divides the members of Las Abejas to this day. Some of these members betrayed the cause by aligning themselves with the state government, which took advantage of the poverty of the population. The government tried to take control of the coffee cooperative, offering subsidies in exchange for abandonment of the cause. This government policy persists to this day.

Another division was recently caused by those who felt entitled to hand-outs because of their victimization. In their weakness, some of these people verbally attacked those non-indigenous who had supported them.

The third wound was unconsciously caused by those of us who supported the Chiapas indigenous. After the massacre and through these two decades, innumerable groups have come in solidarity from both inside and outside Mexico to visit the site of these terrible happenings. They not only offered material help, but also built relationships with Las Abejas. They considered themselves a "human shield" against aggressions in the "low intensity war." Human rights defenders, church groups, and non-government organizations all wished for peace in the region, and in some situations influenced indigenous behavior.

Unfortunately, many indigenous developed an attitude of dependence. They had never imagined that as poor peasants they could be maintained at others' expense. Lacking resources to care for their health, their habitat, and their studies, and trapped in the unending race to fulfill their immediate needs, they did not become self-sustaining. Only the coffee cooperative managed to consolidate. Other projects never got off the ground. The education initiative has made the most progress because of the perseverance of the non-indigenous couple that supports it.

Over the years Las Abejas has received thousands of people who have drawn near to drink from the fount of inspiration at their "sacred ground" of Acteal. Their handmade crafts have been distributed around the world. The dignity of these men and women belonging to the ancient Mayan culture rests in their deeply-rooted Christian faith, never failing in hope. They live their faith in community, sharing and giving themselves selflessly to continue achieving their pacifist ideal.

Even with their open wounds they continue to cry out for justice. They pray and fast, working for peace by issuing communiqués from the tomb of the martyrs. Their struggle is echoed in many other places in Mexico, where we continue to see people disappear and aggressions against groups of workers and peasants. Las Abejas stands in solidarity with these just social causes. They have not accepted a monetary settlement for the victimization they suffered, but stand firmly by their faith and political vision. They continue to demand justice from the Mexican authorities in the face of the impunity and cover-up that have been allowed in the eighteen years since the massacre of Acteal. ⤳

Translated from Spanish by Susan Arnold.

Members of Las Abejas pray outside the chapel in Acteal where the 1997 massacre took place (2013).

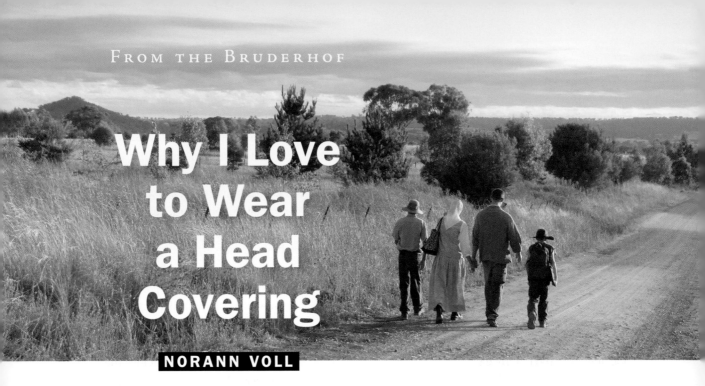

Why I Love to Wear a Head Covering

NORANN VOLL

The author and her family, New South Wales, Australia

I **have walked** through cities and villages, restaurants and rainforests in the United States, Europe, and Australia, and I have always been stared at. That's because I wear a head covering and a long skirt – and, more often than not, I am holding a man's hand.

My husband and I have been married for almost eighteen years, and we love to walk hand in hand. When I hold Chris's hand, we joyfully proclaim that we belong to each other. By the way we dress, I hope we also make it obvious we belong to Jesus – or at least obvious that we don't subscribe to fashion trends.

I've lost track of how many times my clothing and head covering have given me opportunities to tell others about the reason for the hope I have, to witness to just how much I love Jesus. That's one of the blessings of dressing differently.

Of course, many people who wear "normal" clothes are far bolder than I am in reaching out to others and sharing the good news of Jesus. This is not to say that I'm a better person for covering my head or wearing homemade dresses, or that doing so gives me a golden ticket to heaven.

So what motivates me? Head covering and modesty have been longstanding concerns of Jesus' disciples from the very beginning. The apostle Paul, who continued Jesus' example of honoring women, writes to Timothy, "I also want women to dress modestly, with decency and propriety, not with braided hair or gold or pearls or expensive clothes, but with good deeds, appropriate for women who profess to worship God" (1 Tim. 2:9–10), and to the Corinthian church, "that every woman who prays or prophesies with her head uncovered dishonors her head" (1 Cor. 11:5).

I know Christian women the world over bristle about these words. I realize, too, that the account of one person's experience isn't going to change that. So let me be clear that, while those Bible passages certainly inspire me, my desire to cover my head comes not merely from reading the scriptures or early church history but from my own conviction, and the answer to what motivates me is actually pretty simple.

Wearing a head covering and dressing modestly make me feel liberated. For me, it's not an omen of oppression, but a flag of freedom.

It offers freedom, first of all, in the sense of being rightly related to my Creator and enables me to maintain an attitude of permanent worship. I like to think that the twenty minutes I spend prayer-walking my way to work each morning – when I luxuriate in the holiness of God's own house with its great blue sky domed above me and the zebra finches bickering incessantly on the fencerows – are minutes I've stolen from the mirror. I don't wear makeup, and I don't have wardrobe or hairstyle decisions to bog down the start of my day.

Second, it offers freedom from comparison, that ever-lurking "thief of joy," because I am not beholden to any fashion standard, nor am I setting an example that makes another woman feel unworthy.

And, most blessedly, it offers me the freedom to allow the right relationships of other men toward me and, ultimately, freedom from the enslavement of objectification. In other words, by endeavoring to dress and behave in the manner I feel most honors my womanhood, I hope I am inspiring men to behave like true men.

Like a temple adorned from the outside with decorations that denote worthiness, my clothing consecrates, communicates, sets aside, and sets apart. By wearing a head covering, I am making a clear statement to the visible and invisible world that my allegiance is to God.

But having said that, my head covering has not separated me from anyone, or prevented me from forming deep and strong friendships with many amazing women and men the world over. They know that for me it is not about piety or perfectionism, but a reminder of the grace that covers me every day. They respect me because they know that dressing simply gives me a great sense of peace and belonging: belonging to God, and, as a married woman, belonging to one excellent man.

By covering my hair, I'm saying my hairstyle doesn't matter, but my mind, heart, and character do. By covering my body, I'm saying my confidence doesn't come from fashion or fitness, but from a deep sense of knowing I am worthy just for who I am, not what I look like. Wearing a head covering says that I not only accept but love the woman God has created me to be. And it aligns with my belief that dressing with modesty, dressing with the deepest respect for myself, will in turn awaken respect in others.

Of course, I still get stares, and sometimes "You look so beautiful!" or, "Your clothing is just so peaceful." But always, always, I get great questions, and I love the opportunity to tell people why I dress the way I do.

The question I'm most often asked is, "Do you have to?" What I hear is, "Is this *really* your choice?" I fully understand the question, especially as I'm part of a community in which all women wear the same modest style.

The answer is no, I don't have to. I wear what I wear because I choose to, for the reasons mentioned above, and for another reason too: so that my three sons see that the love of Jesus, and the deep love and respect of my husband, are all I need to feel whole. ⤳

Norann Voll is a writer living in Elsmore, New South Wales, Australia. A version of this article appeared on the "Voices" blog at www.bruderhof.com, *the website of the community that publishes* Plough.

Vincent van Gogh

JASON LANDSEL

Jason Landsel is the artist for *Plough's* "Forerunners" series, including the painting opposite.

From outdoor installations to film, music, and even themed hotel rooms, tributes to Vincent van Gogh's art can be found everywhere these days. And no wonder. His aggressive brushstrokes, like those in his most recognized work, *Starry Night,* burst with a wild adrenaline and convey a lust for life. But who was van Gogh? In many ways, he was almost a caricature of the tortured artist. A social outcast who suffered from a long list of mental and physical ailments, some self-inflicted, he shot himself at the age of thirty-seven in a wheat field in Auvers, France.

Born in 1853 to a devout Christian family in the Netherlands, van Gogh was determined to follow in his father's footsteps as a clergyman. Passionate to a fault, his efforts only led to failure and to rejection by the church establishment. However, his missionary work with impoverished coal miners left its mark and gave him a deep empathy for human suffering. At the age of twenty-seven he began to draw and paint seriously. His attempt to serve the church had failed – now he would preach with colors and brush.

Over eight hundred letters, written primarily to his brother and benefactor, Theo, convey van Gogh's journey and development as a person and as an artist. Far from mere mad rantings, they reveal a depth and intelligence, a search for truth. Van Gogh wanted to create a new mode of art that could reach the soul. He wanted his viewers to absorb the explosive life force of the sun, to acknowledge the miraculous cycle of fertility in a freshly plowed field, to see heaven here on earth in the flight of the stars. "One cannot do better than hold on to the thought of God through everything, under all circumstances, at all places, at all times, and try to acquire more knowledge about him, which one can do from the Bible as well as from all other things. It is good to continue believing that everything is more miraculous than one can comprehend, for this is truth," he wrote. "It is good to remain sensitive and humble and tender of heart."

In his book *The Power of Art,* Simon Schama explains the artist's mission to convey the miraculous: "Van Gogh yearned to make painting that was charged with the visionary radiance that had once been supplied by Christianity. Jesus, he wrote, was an artist whose medium had been humanity. Vincent wanted modern art to be a gospel, a bringer of light, that would comfort and redeem through ecstatic witness."

Sadly, during van Gogh's lifetime his color-soaked proclamations were mostly ignored; he sold only one of his approximately nine hundred paintings. "A great fire burns within me, but no one stops to warm themselves at it," he lamented.

Though our culture encourages us to idolize fame and success, van Gogh's story challenges us to consider a different path. He reminds us that in a life lived with passion for the gospel, weakness and failure are not the last word.

> *"I should one day like to show by my work what such an eccentric, such a nobody, has in his heart. That is my ambition, based less on resentment than on love in spite of everything, based more on a feeling of serenity than on passion. Though I am often in the depths of misery, there is still calmness, pure harmony, and music inside me. I see paintings or drawings in the poorest cottages, in the dirtiest corners. And my mind is driven towards these things with an irresistible momentum."*
>
> Vincent van Gogh